BASIC / NOT BORING
SCIENCE SKILLS

LIFE
SCIENCE

Grades 6–8⁺

Inventive Exercises to Sharpen
Skills and Raise Achievement

Series Concept & Development
by Imogene Forte & Marjorie Frank
Exercises by Marjorie Frank

Incentive Publications, Inc.
Nashville, Tennessee

About the cover:
Bound resist, or tie dye, is the most ancient known method of fabric surface design. The brilliance of the basic tie dye design on this cover reflects the possibilities that emerge from the mastery of basic skills.

Illustrated by Kathleen Bullock
Cover art by Mary Patricia Deprez, dba Tye Dye Mary®
Cover design by Marta Drayton, Joe Shibley, and W. Paul Nance
Edited by Anna Quinn

ISBN 0-86530-374-6

1   2   3   4   5   6   7   8   9   10   07   06   05   04
PRINTED IN THE UNITED STATES OF AMERICA
www.incentivepublications.com

TABLE OF CONTENTS

INTRODUCTION . . . Celebrate Basic Life Science Skills 7

Skills Checklist for Life Science 8

SKILLS EXERCISES 9

That's Life! . . . (Characteristics of Living Things) 10

Osmosis Is Not a Disease . . . (Cell Processes) 11

A Cell-a-Bration . . . (Cell Structure) 12

Welcome to the Kingdom . . . (Classification of Life) 14

A Visit from a Virus . . . (Viruses & Monerans) 15

Strange Choice of Friends . . . (Fungi & Protists) 16

Plant Parts, Inc. . . . (Plant Structure) 17

Plant Antics . . . (Plant Processes) 18

What Do Bees Know? . . . (Flower Parts/Angiosperm Reproduction) 19

Would You Sleep on a Monocot? . . . (Plant Facts & Vocabulary) 20

Bones or No Bones? . . . (Vertebrates & Invertebrates) 22

A Side View . . . (Animal Symmetry) 23

File into Phyla . . . (Animal Classification) 24

Of Worms, Jellyfish, & Sponges . . . (Simple Invertebrates) 26

It's Hard to Ignore a Squid . . . (Mollusks & Echinoderms) 27

Outnumbered! . . . (Arthropods) 28

Confusion in the Web . . . (Arachnids) 29

Bugs by the Millions . . . (Insects) 30

The Most Amazing Changes . . . (Metamorphosis in Insects) 31

Blood That's Cold . . . (Fish, Reptiles, & Amphibians) 32

Blood That's Warm . . . (Birds & Mammals) 33

Class Assignments . . . (Vertebrate Classes) 34

Backbone Required . . . (Vertebrate Facts) 35

Behaving Like Animals . . . (Animal Behavior) 36

Scales for a Crocodile? . . . (Animal-Related Vocabulary) 37

The Habitat Habit . . . (Habitats) 38

Something's Wrong Here . . . (Habitats) 39

Home, Home on the Biome . . . (Biomes) 40

Everybody's in a Chain . . . (Food Chains) 42

What's What in the Ecosystem? . . . (Ecosystems) 43

Relationships in the Ecosystem . . . (Ecosystems) 44

Cycle Circles . . . (Natural Cycles) 45

Eco-Talk . . . (Ecology) 46

How Resourceful Are You? . . . (Natural Resources) 47

Under the Microscope . . . (Microscope Use) 48

APPENDIX 49

Glossary 50

Protist, Moneran, & Fungus Kingdoms 53

Plant Kingdom 54

Animal Kingdom 55

Life Science Skills Test 57

Skills Test Answer Key 61

Answers 62

CELEBRATE BASIC LIFE SCIENCE SKILLS

Basic does not mean boring! There certainly is nothing dull about . . .

... visiting with viruses

... taking a look at the stuff inside cells

... tracking down bones in creatures

... learning who's eating whom in the ecosystem

... wondering why animals stand on their heads or play dead

... getting to know what's inside squids & slugs & sea urchins

... becoming an expert on ticks and tarantulas

... finding out who's got fake feet and why

... knowing what's inside a frog

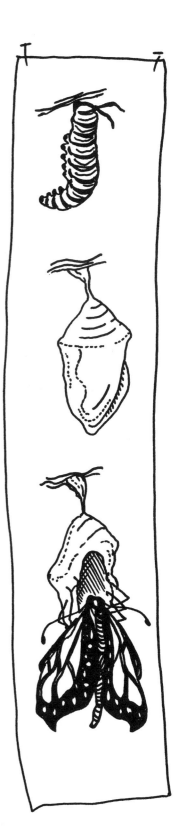

The idea of celebrating the basics—enjoying and improving science skills—is just what it sounds like. The pages that follow are full of exercises for students that will help to review and strengthen specific, basic skills in the content area of life science. This is not just another "fill-in-the-blanks" way to learn. These interesting activities will put students to work applying a rich variety of the most important facts about many aspects of life science while enjoying fun and challenging activities about plants, animals, ecosystems, and ecology.

The pages in this book can be used in many ways:

• for individual students to sharpen a particular skill

• with a small group needing to relearn or strengthen a skill

• as an instructional tool for teaching a skill to any size group

• by students working on their own

• by students working under the direction of an adult

Each page may be used to introduce a new skill or content area, reinforce a skill, or assess a student's ability to perform a skill. And, there's more than just the great student activities! You'll also find a hearty appendix of resources helpful for students and teachers—including a ready-to-use test for assessing these life science content skills.

As students take on the challenges of these adventures with living things, they will sharpen their mastery of basic skills and have a good time while they do it. And as you watch them check off the basic life science skills they've strengthened, you can celebrate with them!

SKILLS CHECKLIST FOR
LIFE SCIENCE

✔	SKILL	PAGE(S)
	Define characteristics of living things	10
	Label and describe structural parts of plant and animal cells	12-13
	Describe and distinguish between cell processes	11
	Describe the system of classification of life	14, 16, 24, 25, 34
	Describe and distinguish between simple organisms	15, 16
	Identify features of plant structure and explain their functions	17, 19
	Define, describe, and distinguish between plant processes	18
	Identify flower parts and their functions	19
	Describe pollination and fertilization in angiosperms	19
	Define and use vocabulary terms related to plants	20, 21
	Describe the system of classification of animals	22, 24-30, 32, 33
	Describe and distinguish between different kinds of symmetry	23
	Identify characteristics of different animal phyla	24-28, 32-35
	Identify characteristics of simple invertebrates	26
	Identify characteristics of mollusks and echinoderms	27
	Identify & distinguish among characteristics of different arthropods	28, 29, 30
	Identify characteristics of arachnids	29
	Identify characteristics of insects	30
	Describe complete and incomplete metamorphosis in insects	31
	Define characteristics of vertebrates	22, 32-35
	Define characteristics of cold-blooded vertebrates	32
	Define characteristics of warm-blooded vertebrates	33
	Identify terms and characteristics related to animal behavior	36
	Define and use vocabulary terms related to animals	37
	Describe, identify, and give examples of habitats	38, 39
	Define and identify characteristics of different biomes	40, 41
	Explain the relationships in food chains	42
	Explain concepts related to ecosystems	43
	Identify a variety of relationships in ecosystems	43, 44
	Explain CO_2–O_2, nitrogen, and water cycles	45
	Define and use vocabulary terms related to ecology	46
	Identify concepts related to the use of natural resources	47
	Identify the parts of a light microscope and their functions	48

LIFE SCIENCE

Skills Exercises

THAT'S LIFE!

How do you tell that something is living? You just check to see if the "thing" has the 7 characteristics of all living things.

I. Each picture here represents one of the characteristics. Label each picture with a phrase that tells what characteristic of life it shows.

II. The page below shows a student's notes from her science log. She is writing some things she's learned about the characteristics of living things. Fill in the blanks with the missing words. (Choose from the box at the bottom of the page.)

1

_____

2

_____

3

_____

4

_____

5

_____

6

_____

7

_____

Each living thing is called an _____ . The basic unit of structure and function in an organism is the _____ . Three main elements that make up living things are _____ , _____ , and _____ . Water makes up about _____ of most organisms. It helps to _____ food through the organism and also helps remove _____ . Oxygen is used by organisms to help release _____ from food. A trait that helps an organism survive and change to fit its environment is called an _____ . A _____ is a group of cells with similar shape and function that perform a specific job. An _____ is a group of tissues that work together to perform a life activity. A _____ is a group of organs that work together to carry on life activities.

(blanks numbered 8, 9, 10, 11, 12, 13, 14, 15, 16, 17, 18, 19, 20)

tissue	cell	circulate	carbon dioxide
energy	organism	water	adaptation
fertilization	hydrogen	70%	system
nitrogen	oxygen	organ	50%
carbon	30%	wastes	digestion

Name _____

10

OSMOSIS IS NOT A DISEASE

Osmosis may sound like a disease. But it is not! It's the name of one of the processes that occupy the lives of living cells. Ozzy Mosis, the budding young scientist, needs help sorting out these processes. For each question, choose one of the words below that names the process. (A word may be used more than once.)

homeostasis   **mitosis**

osmosis   **diffusion**

active transport

cell division   **metabolism**

plasmolysis   **respiration**

_____ 1. Crowded particles in water move from their tight space to a place where there is more room. What's going on?

_____ 2. Celery stalk cells go limp when water diffuses out. Why?

_____ 3. A cell's nucleus divides into 2 nuclei so 2 new cells can form. What process is this?

_____ 4. Cells in a plant root drink in water through the cell membrane. What process is going on?

_____ 5. The growth, repair, and use of food in your body are all part of what cell process?

_____ 6. Single cells split into 2 cells. What process is this?

_____ 7. Cells break down food in a chemical reaction that releases energy. What process is this?

_____ 8. During exercise, your body sweats to cool off so its temperature doesn't get too high. What process is this?

_____ 9. Energy is used to move particles from a place of lower to higher concentration. What cell process is this?

_____ 10. Your body shivers to warm up muscles when you sit on an iceberg in your swimsuit. What cell process is this?

_____ 11. What process is the opposite of active transport?

_____ 12. What process happens in the cell before cell division can take place?

_____ 13. The sum of all chemical changes that occur in an organism is what process?

Name _____

A CELL-A-BRATION

If you know all the parts of a cell, you can celebrate along with these partying cells. Show what you know by doing the following:

I. Label each cell part on the next page (page 13) with its correct name.
(See names on List 1 below.)

II. Label each cell correctly as **animal cell** or **plant cell.**

III. Match each cell part (below) with its function on List 2. Write the letter of the cell part in front of the number of the matching descriptive phrase.

List 2

_____ 1. controls chlorophyll to help cell trap light to make food

_____ 2. tube network in cytoplasm where cell substances are made

_____ 3. controls movement of materials in and out of the nucleus

_____ 4. controls cell activities

_____ 5. contains cell materials

_____ 6. surrounds plant cell; gives shape and support to the cell

_____ 7. proteins are made in these

_____ 8. rod-shaped bodies that release energy for cell use

_____ 9. bodies that store and release chemicals for cell use

_____ 10. controls movement of materials in and out of the cell

_____ 11. holds the code that controls cell

_____ 12. stores water and dissolved materials in plant cells

List 1

A endoplasmic reticulum (ER)

B nucleus

C nuclear membrane

D ribosomes

E cytoplasm

F chromosomes

G cell membrane

H mitochondria

I Golgi bodies

J vacuole

K chloroplast

L cell wall

Use with page 13.

Name _____

CELL DIAGRAMS

Use with page 12.

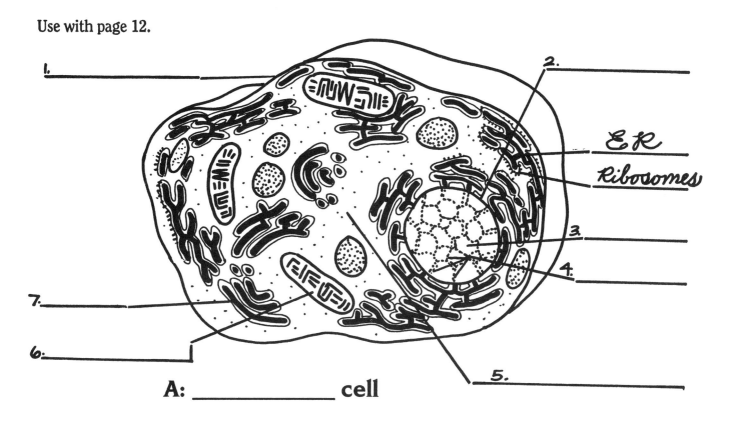

1. _____

2. _____

E.R

Ribosomes

3. _____

4. _____

7. _____

6. _____

5. _____

A: _____ **cell**

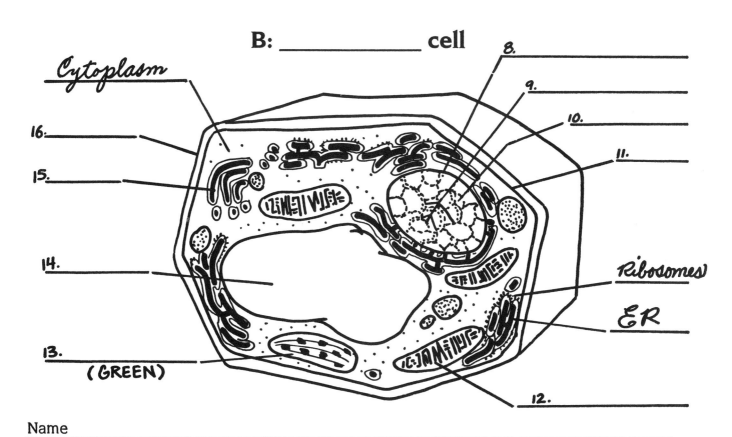

B: _____ **cell**

Cytoplasm

8. _____

9. _____

10. _____

11. _____

16. _____

15. _____

Ribosomes

E.R

14. _____

13. _____

(GREEN)

12. _____

Name _____

13

WELCOME TO THE KINGDOM

Living things are classified into five kingdoms. Has the mighty Leo named them correctly? Cross out any incorrect labels and write in the correct ones. Then, write the correct kingdom next to each phrase that describes one of the characteristics of its members (items 6-15). Some will have more than one answer.

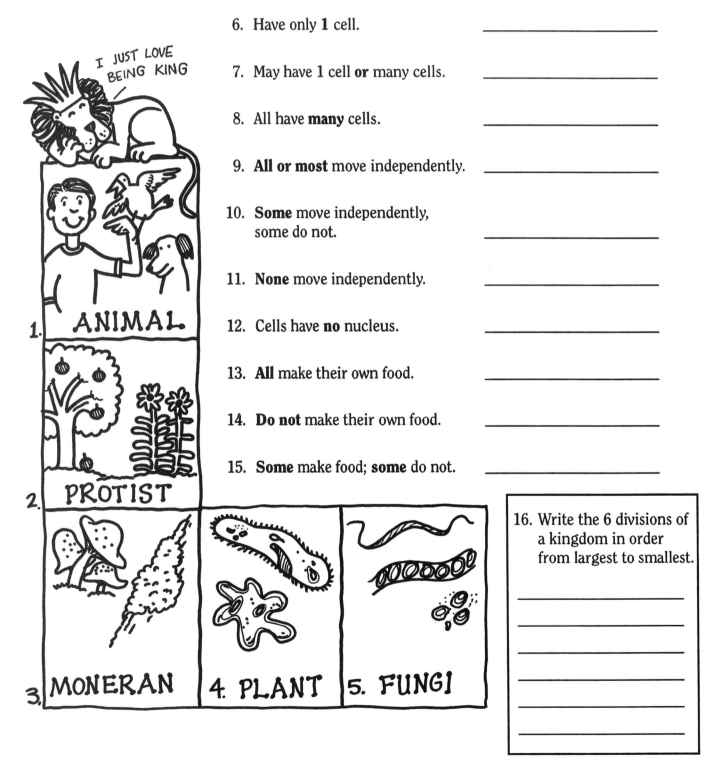

I JUST LOVE BEING KING

1. ANIMAL

2. PROTIST

3. MONERAN

4. PLANT

5. FUNGI

6. Have only **1** cell. _____

7. May have **1** cell **or** many cells. _____

8. All have **many** cells. _____

9. **All or most** move independently. _____

10. **Some** move independently, some do not. _____

11. **None** move independently. _____

12. Cells have **no** nucleus. _____

13. **All** make their own food. _____

14. **Do not** make their own food. _____

15. **Some** make food; **some** do not. _____

16. Write the 6 divisions of a kingdom in order from largest to smallest.

_____
_____
_____
_____
_____
_____

Name _____

A VISIT FROM A VIRUS

You've probably been visited by a virus or some bacteria, so you are qualified to answer these questions. Write your answers on the lines preceeding the questions.

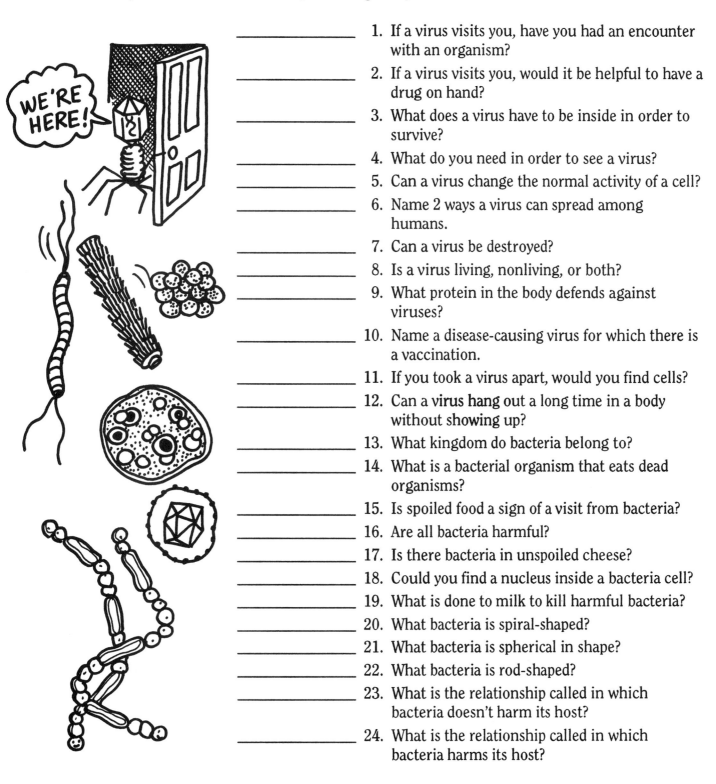

1. If a virus visits you, have you had an encounter with an organism?

2. If a virus visits you, would it be helpful to have a drug on hand?

3. What does a virus have to be inside in order to survive?

4. What do you need in order to see a virus?

5. Can a virus change the normal activity of a cell?

6. Name 2 ways a virus can spread among humans.

7. Can a virus be destroyed?

8. Is a virus living, nonliving, or both?

9. What protein in the body defends against viruses?

10. Name a disease-causing virus for which there is a vaccination.

11. If you took a virus apart, would you find cells?

12. Can a **virus hang** out a long time in a body without **showing** up?

13. What kingdom do bacteria belong to?

14. What is a bacterial organism that eats dead organisms?

15. Is spoiled food a sign of a visit from bacteria?

16. Are all bacteria harmful?

17. Is there bacteria in unspoiled cheese?

18. Could you find a nucleus inside a bacteria cell?

19. What is done to milk to kill harmful bacteria?

20. What bacteria is spiral-shaped?

21. What bacteria is spherical in shape?

22. What bacteria is rod-shaped?

23. What is the relationship called in which bacteria doesn't harm its host?

24. What is the relationship called in which bacteria harms its host?

Name

Basic Skills/Life Science 6-8+

STRANGE CHOICE OF FRIENDS

Fungi and protists don't get a lot of respect from most people. They are not exactly plants or animals. But Lorena thinks they're rather interesting characters. So she's listing impressive facts about protists and fungi. But is she right? Use your knowledge about protists and fungi to decide if each thing she's written is true (T) or false (F).

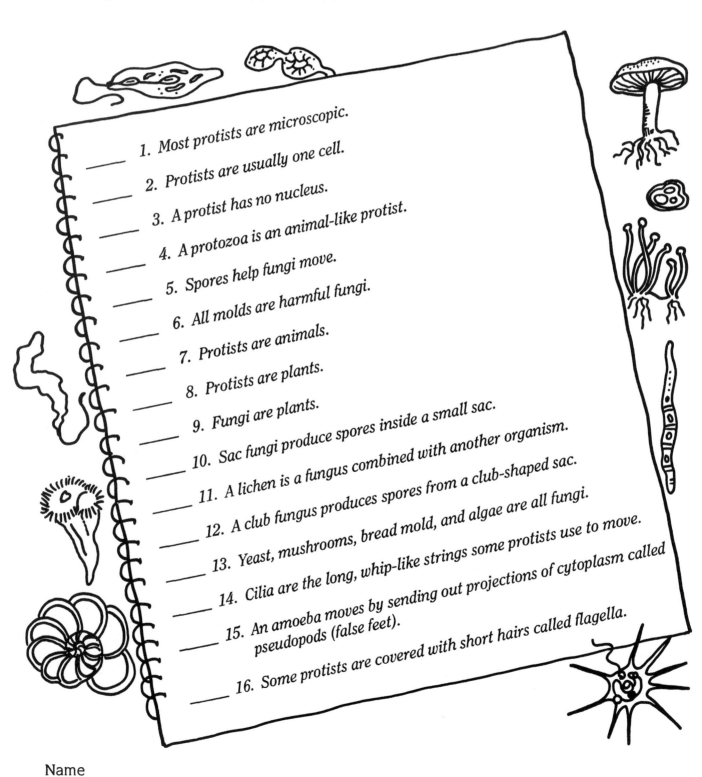

1. Most protists are microscopic.

2. Protists are usually one cell.

3. A protist has no nucleus.

4. A protozoa is an animal-like protist.

5. Spores help fungi move.

6. All molds are harmful fungi.

7. Protists are animals.

8. Protists are plants.

9. Fungi are plants.

10. Sac fungi produce spores inside a small sac.

11. A lichen is a fungus combined with another organism.

12. A club fungus produces spores from a club-shaped sac.

13. Yeast, mushrooms, bread mold, and algae are all fungi.

14. Cilia are the long, whip-like strings some protists use to move.

15. An amoeba moves by sending out projections of cytoplasm called pseudopods (false feet).

16. Some protists are covered with short hairs called flagella.

Name _____

PLANT PARTS, INC.

Cat A. Pilar tried going into the auto parts business. But she had a bit of trouble getting customers to believe she could replace a carburetor or repair brake systems. So she switched to plant parts. Here's a list of broken parts her customers have brought in. Tell what each part is by writing a brief description.

1. leaf _____

2. xylem _____

3. taproot system _____

4. epidermis _____

5. cuticle _____

6. phloem _____

7. vessels _____

8. cambium _____

9. blade _____

10. stomata _____

11. petiole _____

12. fibrous root system _____

13. root hairs _____

14. roots _____

FLOWER PETALS? OR BIKE PEDALS?

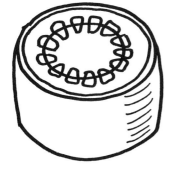

A.

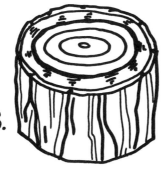

B.

Woodruff Woodchuck brought in these two stems to be fixed.

15. Which stem is woody? _____

16. Which is herbaceous? _____

Name _____

PLANT ANTICS

So you thought plants just stood around all day doing nothing? Not so! They breathe, eat, grow, make food, sweat, and move stuff around inside all the time. There are four plant processes pictured here. Use the phrases below to help you write a description of each of these four processes. You might use some of the phrases in more than one place.

PHOTOSYNTHESIS:

TRANSPIRATION:

RESPIRATION:

GAS EXCHANGE:

- tiny openings called stomata
- opposite of photosynthesis
- sugar and oxygen are produced
- green plants trap light
- water vapor is lost through stomata
- stomata open during the day
- takes place in cells with chlorophyll
- oxygen, carbon dioxide, & water vapor
- energy is released from food

- light energy is used to make food
- gases are lost by diffusion
- water and carbon dioxide are produced
- stomata are closed at night
- carbon dioxide and water combine
- energy is stored in food
- light energy used for chemical reactions
- opposite of respiration

Name

WHAT DO BEES KNOW?

This know-it-all bee thinks he can describe the pollination and fertilization that takes place in this flower. Does he know as much as he thinks? Read through his explanation and find the errors. Cross out and fix anything that is not correct.

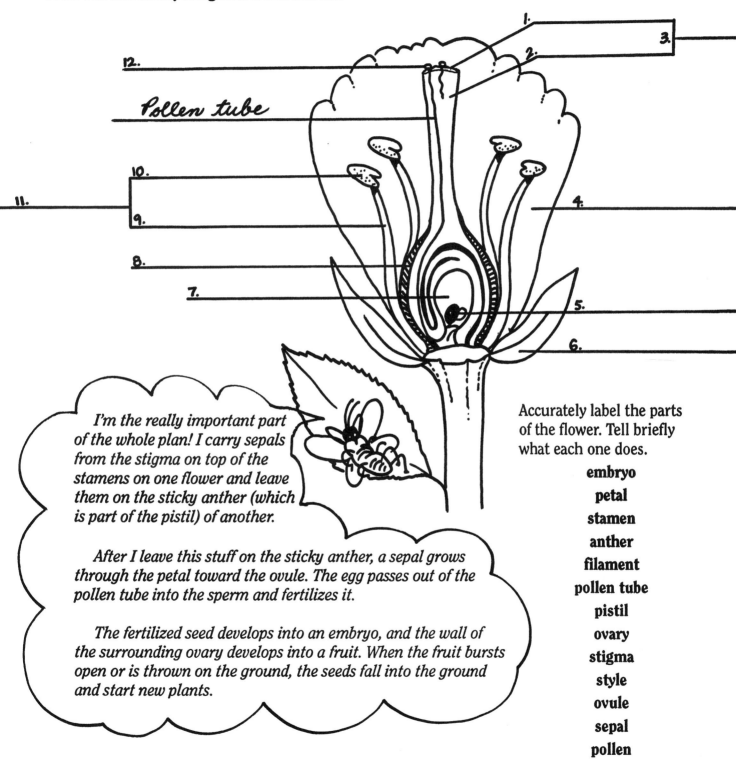

12. _Pollen tube_

I'm the really important part of the whole plan! I carry sepals from the stigma on top of the stamens on one flower and leave them on the sticky anther (which is part of the pistil) of another.

After I leave this stuff on the sticky anther, a sepal grows through the petal toward the ovule. The egg passes out of the pollen tube into the sperm and fertilizes it.

The fertilized seed develops into an embryo, and the wall of the surrounding ovary develops into a fruit. When the fruit bursts open or is thrown on the ground, the seeds fall into the ground and start new plants.

Accurately label the parts of the flower. Tell briefly what each one does.

embryo
petal
stamen
anther
filament
pollen tube
pistil
ovary
stigma
style
ovule
sepal
pollen

Name

WOULD YOU SLEEP ON A MONOCOT?

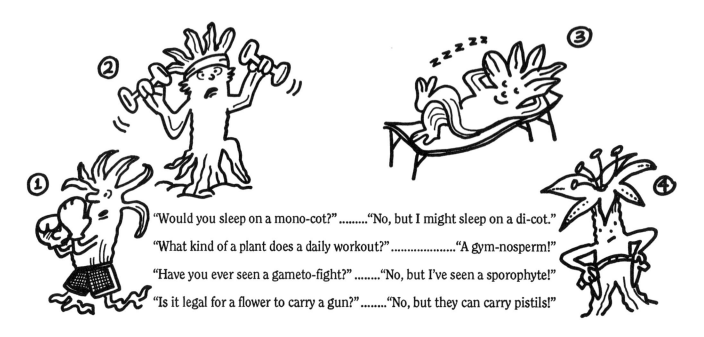

"Would you sleep on a mono-cot?" .... "No, but I might sleep on a di-cot."

"What kind of a plant does a daily workout?" .... "A gym-nosperm!"

"Have you ever seen a gameto-fight?" .... "No, but I've seen a sporophyte!"

"Is it legal for a flower to carry a gun?" .... "No, but they can carry pistils!"

The vocabulary terms on the plant on page 21 are all answers to plant "riddles" on this page. Write the number of each of the following questions on the matching answer leaf on page 21.

1. I come in green, brown, and red, and have no roots, stems, or leaves.
2. Water vapor is lost from leaves through me.
3. I anchor plants in soil.
4. You'll find me holding a moss or liverwort in the ground.
5. I am not found in mosses, algae, or liverworts.
6. Conifers hide their seeds in me.
7. When you eat an apple, you are eating me.
8. Plants use me from the atmosphere to make food.
9. I'm the female reproductive organ of an angiosperm.
10. I'm the reason plants are green.
11. My flower petal parts come in sets of 4 or 5.
12. Visit me if you're looking for a frond.
13. I'm a seed plant that has no fruit.
14. I am formed from sporophytes.
15. I am formed from gametophytes.

16. I'm a growing young plant that rests during dormancy.
17. Plants get me from the soil.
18. My flower parts come in sets of 3.
19. I am the young leaves inside the embryo of a seed.
20. I have soft, green stems.
21. You're eating me when you eat a cob of corn.
22. Plants get nitrogen from me.
23. This is how some plants are like your circulatory system.
24. I cause production of food using light.
25. We are the male reproductive organs of angiosperms.
26. Plants add me to the atmosphere.
27. I grow, reproduce, and die within one season.
28. Chlorophyll traps me.
29. The purpose of seeds is to produce more of me.
30. I'm a plant with no vessels.

Use with page 21.

Name

Use with page 20.

A   a pistil
B   an algae
D   a plant embryo
O   a cotyledon
E   herbaceous
H   a gymnosperm
R   stomata
G   oxygen
Q   vessels
C   a fern
F   nonvascular
P   carbon dioxide
L   photosynthesis
N   light energy
M   Both have vessels.
U   an annual
X   stamens
T   endosperm
Y   nitrogen
S   gametes
Z   spores
ZZ   an angiosperm
V   new plants
BB   chlorophyll
AA   cones
W   soil
XX   a rhizoid
I   roots
J   a monocot
K   a dicot

Name

BONES OR NO BONES?

Some animals have them. Some do not. A backbone may not seem like a big deal to you, but it is a major feature in the classification of animal species. Look at all the characteristics and animals in this list. Write the number of each one where it belongs—either in the BONES (vertebrates) or the NO BONES (invertebrates) category.

1. salamander
2. 95% of known species
3. toad
4. phylum chordata
5. snail
6. coral
7. pelican
8. turtle
9. soft bodies
10. internal skeleton
11. snake
12. sponge
13. tarantula
14. humans
15. exoskeletons
16. earthworm
17. wasp
18. clam
19. goldfish
20. ostrich
21. dolphin
22. spinal cord
23. skeletons made of bone
24. spider
25. slug
26. whale
27. skeletons made of cartilage
28. shark
29. closed circulatory systems
30. fly
31. zebra
32. crocodile

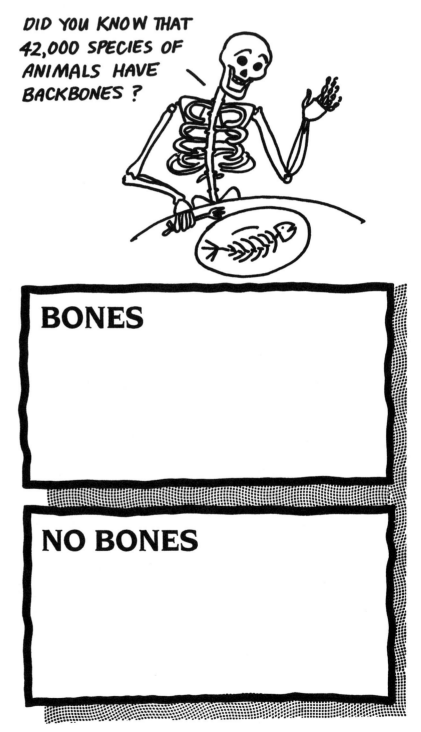

DID YOU KNOW THAT 42,000 SPECIES OF ANIMALS HAVE BACKBONES?

BONES

NO BONES

Name

A SIDE VIEW

Bertram Bi Olly Gist wants to classify these animals according to their **symmetry.** Help him out. Label each animal with *B* for **bilateral**, *R* for **radial**, or *N* for **no symmetry**.

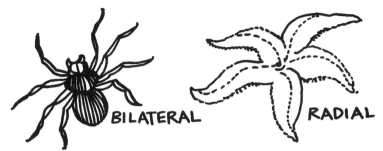

BILATERAL RADIAL

NO SYMMETRY

Symmetry is a similarity or likeness of two parts.

An organism with **bilateral symmetry** has two sides or parts that are alike.

An organism with **radial symmetry** has an arrangement of similar parts around a central axis like spokes of a wheel.

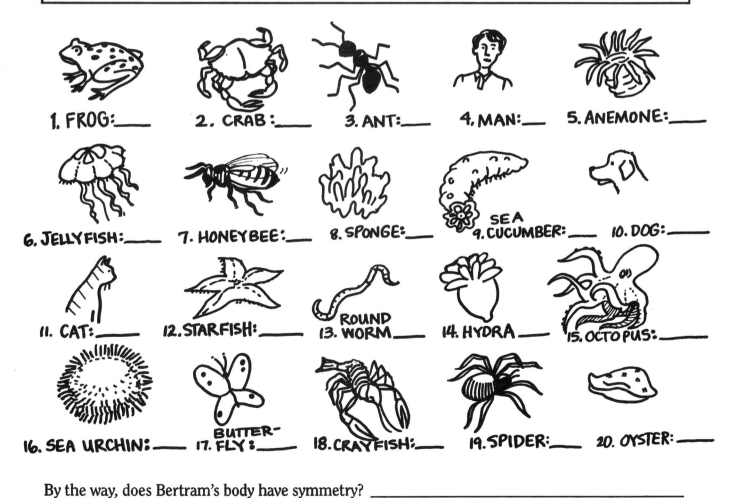

1. FROG:____   2. CRAB:____   3. ANT:____   4. MAN:____   5. ANEMONE:____

6. JELLYFISH:____   7. HONEYBEE:____   8. SPONGE:____   9. SEA CUCUMBER:____   10. DOG:____

11. CAT:____   12. STARFISH:____   13. ROUND WORM____   14. HYDRA____   15. OCTOPUS:____

16. SEA URCHIN:____   17. BUTTER-FLY:____   18. CRAYFISH:____   19. SPIDER:____   20. OYSTER:____

By the way, does Bertram's body have symmetry? _____

Name _____

FILE INTO PHYLA

A **phylum** is kind of like a file. It is a way to group animals with similar characteristics together. There are many different animal **phyla.** The nine major phyla are represented by animals pictured on the next page (page 25). Your job is to make sure that Zak (the zookeeper) has 1 or more animals for each phylum in his "file." Write the name of each animal onto the correct file. Also, find the description on page 25 which matches each phylum, and write the letter on the file.

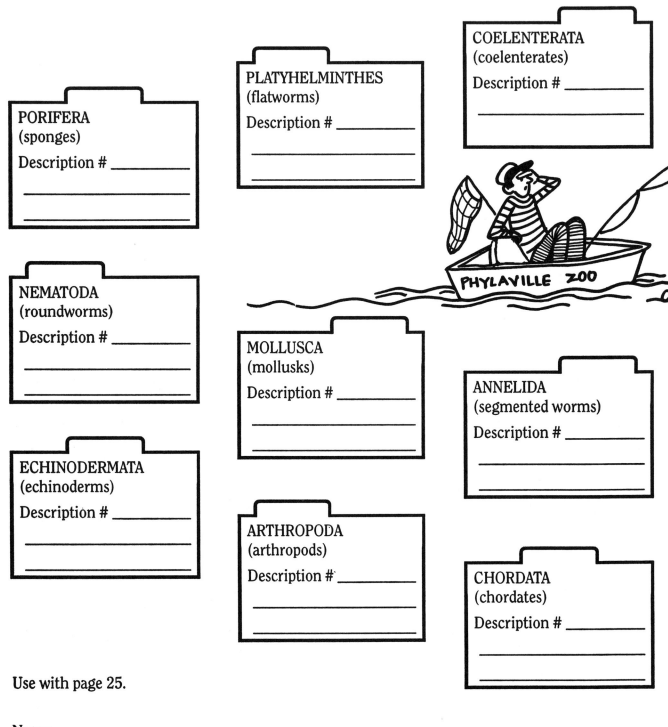

COELENTERATA
(coelenterates)

Description # _____

_____

PLATYHELMINTHES
(flatworms)

Description # _____

_____

PORIFERA
(sponges)

Description # _____

_____

NEMATODA
(roundworms)

Description # _____

_____

MOLLUSCA
(mollusks)

Description # _____

_____

ANNELIDA
(segmented worms)

Description # _____

_____

ECHINODERMATA
(echinoderms)

Description # _____

_____

ARTHROPODA
(arthropods)

Description # _____

_____

CHORDATA
(chordates)

Description # _____

_____

Use with page 25.

Name

Use with page 24.

C. spiny or leathery skin; radial symmetry

GULL

HAWK

E. body divided into sections; jointed legs

G. body divided into segments

H. flat body

BEE

FROG

B. soft bodies, mostly with shell-like coverings

ANT

EARTHWORM

SHRIMP

A. thick sack of cells with pores, chambers, and canals

OCTOPUS

F. internal skeleton; specialized body systems

JELLYFISH

RAY

I. round body

D. central cavity and mouth; most have tentacles

TAPEWORM

CLAM

HOOKWORM

BRISTLEWORM

ELEPHANT SPONGE

SEA URCHIN

Name

OF WORMS, JELLYFISH, & SPONGES

If animals are simple, it ought to be a simple job for you to describe them—right?
These are five of the simpler invertebrate phyla:

coelenterates • sponges • flatworms • roundworms • segmented worms

Determine to which phylum each pictured invertebrate belongs. Label each one. Then, use the space to write everything you know or can find out about characteristics of animals in that phylum.

1

jellyfish

2

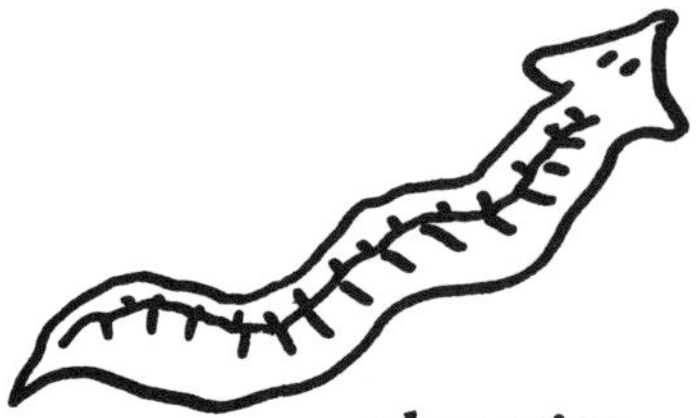

planarian

3

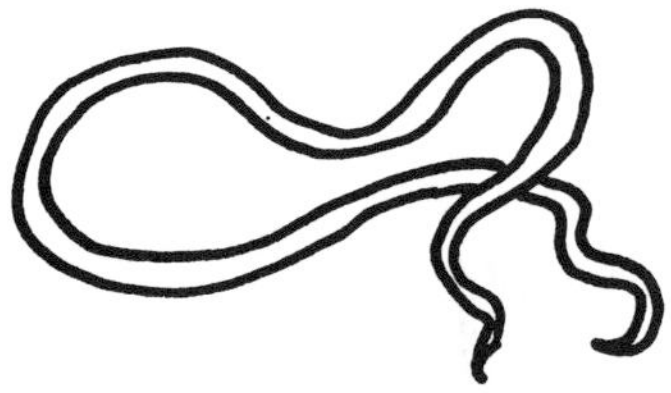

hookworm

4

bristleworm

5

velvet sponge

Name

IT'S HARD TO IGNORE A SQUID

Have you ever have eaten a clam or oyster? Met up with an octopus or squid? Picked up a slug? If so, you've had the honor of knowing a **mollusk.** If you have ever admired a starfish, run into a sea urchin, or collected sand dollars, you've made the acquaintance of an **echinoderm.** Mollusks and echinoderms are animals that many people love to admire, watch, or eat. Some people go so far as to kiss slugs.

I. For each characteristic listed below, write **M** if the characteristic is true of mollusks, **E** if it is true of echinoderms, or **B** if it is true of both.

_____ 1. have a water vascular system for moving and getting food

_____ 2. have bilateral symmetry

_____ 3. have a circulatory system and heart

_____ 4. usually have a hard outer shell

_____ 5. often have tentacles

_____ 6. have a spiny or leathery covering

_____ 7. are invertebrates

_____ 8. all live in salt water

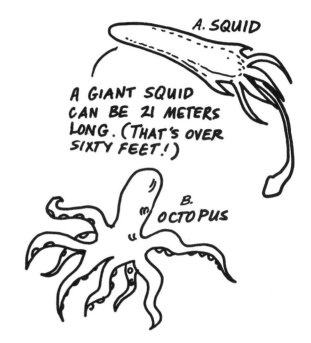

A GIANT SQUID CAN BE 21 METERS LONG. (THAT'S OVER SIXTY FEET!)

A. SQUID

B. OCTOPUS

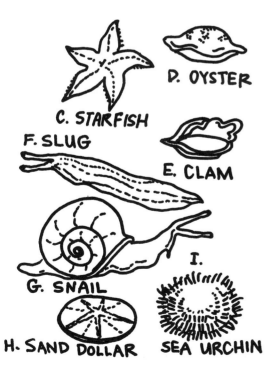

C. STARFISH

D. OYSTER

F. SLUG

E. CLAM

G. SNAIL

H. SAND DOLLAR

I. SEA URCHIN

_____ 9. (some) live attached to rocks

_____ 10. have radial symmetry

_____ 11. have soft bodies

_____ 12. (some) live on land; some live in water

_____ 13. (some) have a thick, muscular "foot" for movement

_____ 14. have spines extending out of their bodies

_____ 15. (most) move slowly by attaching tube-like feet to things and pulling themselves along

_____ 16. are cold-blooded

II. Label each animal on this page **M** for mollusk or **E** for echinoderm.

Name _____

OUTNUMBERED!

What phylum outnumbers all other kinds of animals put together? What phylum has 1500 different species just in your backyard garden? **Arthropods!** They're everywhere!

Look at the characteristics and animals below. Decide whether each characteristic is true of all arthropods or just of one specific class of arthropods. If the characteristic applies to all arthropods, write its letter in the box that says **ALL.** Otherwise, write its letter in the box for its class. (Some are true of more than one class.) Determine the class in which each animal belongs. Write its letter in the appropriate box.

ALL ARTHROPODS

MILLIPEDES

CENTIPEDES

CRUSTACEANS

ARACHNIDS

INSECTS

A. gills

B. 3 pair of legs

C. flat, segmented body

D. 3 body sections

E.

F. jointed legs

G. no antennae

H. exoskeleton

I.

J. 1 pair of legs per segment

K. 1 pair antennae

L. shed exoskeleton periodically by molting

M.

N. 4 pair of legs

O. round, segmented body

P. 2 body sections

Q.

R. 2 pair of antennae

S. bodies divided into sections

T. very hard, flexible exoskeleton

U. 2 pair of legs per segment

V. poison claws on first segment

W. many have 1 or 2 pair of wings

X. mandibles in mouth for chewing

Name

CONFUSION IN THE WEB

Some people think that spiders are insects. They are not! They belong to a class of the arthropod phylum called **arachnids.** Some of the animals caught in this web are arachnids, and others aren't. Answer the questions in the boxes to show what you know about arachnids.

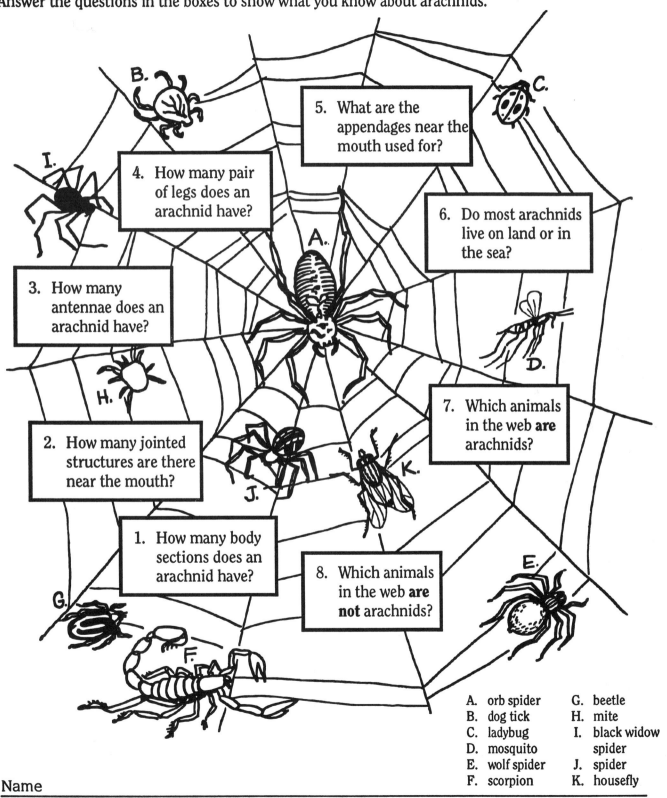

5. What are the appendages near the mouth used for?

4. How many pair of legs does an arachnid have?

6. Do most arachnids live on land or in the sea?

3. How many antennae does an arachnid have?

7. Which animals in the web **are** arachnids?

2. How many jointed structures are there near the mouth?

1. How many body sections does an arachnid have?

8. Which animals in the web **are not** arachnids?

A. orb spider
B. dog tick
C. ladybug
D. mosquito
E. wolf spider
F. scorpion
G. beetle
H. mite
I. black widow spider
J. spider
K. housefly

Name

BUGS BY THE MILLIONS

Did you know that almost 1 million different species of insects have been given names and descriptions? (How would you like to be the person who has to write down all these?) There are, obviously, far more insects than any other class of animals. How much do you know about these millions of bugs that belong to this exclusive class?

I. Tell whether each statement is true (T) or false (F) about insects.

___ 1. They have 2 body parts.
___ 2. They have 3 pair of legs.
___ 3. They have 1 pair of antennae.
___ 4. All insects are harmful.
___ 5. They have an open
     circulatory system.
___ 6. They have no antennae.

___ 7. They have 4 pair of legs.
___ 8. They have 2 pair of antennae.
___ 9. Many have 1 or 2 pair of wings.
___ 10. Some are helpful in pollinating flowers.
___ 11. They are the only invertebrates that can fly.
___ 12. Their body sections are: head, thorax, abdomen.
___ 13. Air enters their bodies through spiracles.

II. Tell which creatures in Kate's collection are NOT insects.

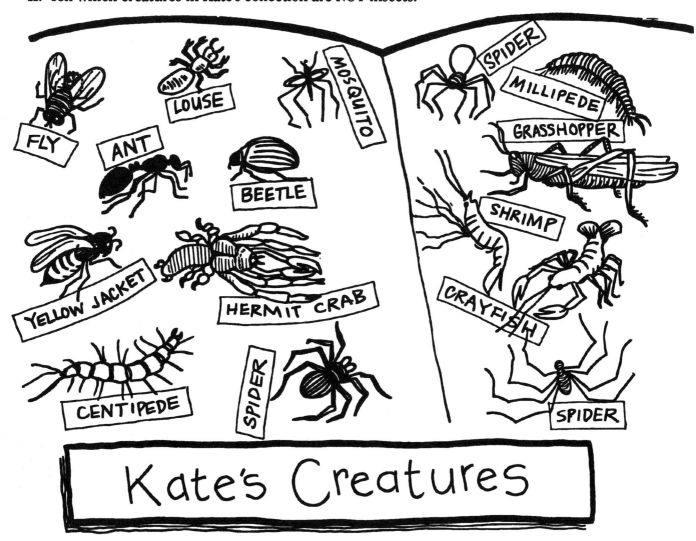

Kate's Creatures

Name

THE MOST AMAZING CHANGES

Imagine starting life as one kind of creature, then changing into something totally different when you become an adult! This is what happens to many insects. An amazing process called **metamorphosis** changes animals from one form into another right before your very eyes. Review what you know about complete metamorphosis and incomplete metamorphosis.

1. Define metamorphosis. _____
_____

2. Name the 4 stages of development in complete metamorphosis.

    1. _____   3. _____
    2. _____   4. _____

3. Describe the process of incomplete metamorphosis. _____
_____

4. Name 2 insects that undergo complete metamorphosis. _____
_____

5. Name 2 insects that undergo incomplete metamorphosis. _____
_____

6. Describe molting. _____
_____

7. Which example shows complete metamorphosis? _____

8. Which example shows incomplete metamorphosis? _____

Label the stages of metamorphosis in the butterfly and the grasshopper.

Monarch Butterfly _____

Grasshopper _____

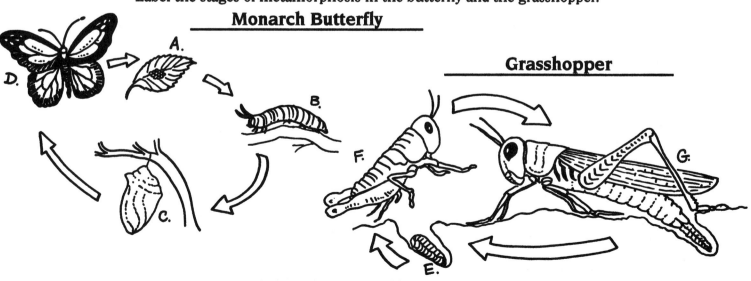

BLOOD THAT'S COLD

Besides a skeleton, blood is the major thing that an eel, a turtle, and a toad have in common. Tell what it means to be cold-blooded. Then fill in the missing information about these cold-blooded classes of animals—fish, reptiles, and amphibians.

Explain "cold-blooded." _____

_____

_____

Label each animal pictured as
F (fish),
R (reptile), or
A (amphibian).

_____ 1 are cold-blooded vertebrates which live in _____ 2. They use _____ 3 to get oxygen from water and have 4-chambered hearts. There are _____ 4 different kinds of animals in this class. Those with sucker-like mouths, such as lampreys, are called _____ 5 fish. Sharks are _____ 6 fish because their skeletons are made of cartilage. _____ 7 fish have skeletons made of bones and have hinged jaws and fins. Young fish hatch from _____ 8. Two examples of this class are _____ 9 and _____ 10.

_____ 11 live part of their lives on _____ 12 and part in _____ 13. They return to _____ 14 to reproduce and lay eggs, but as adults, they live mostly on _____ 15. They have _____ 16 skin with no scales. They breathe _____ 17; though some have _____ 18 for breathing in water. Some change appearance as they _____ 19. The young _____ 20 from eggs. Their hearts have _____ 21 chambers. Two examples of this class are _____ 22 and _____ 23.

_____ 24 breathe _____ 25 and live mostly on _____ 26. Most have long bodies and four legs. Their bodies are covered with _____ 27. They have _____ 28 –chambered hearts. The young are hatched from _____ 29. Two examples of this class are _____ 30 and _____ 31.

Name _____

BLOOD THAT'S WARM

You're not the only species with warm blood. Thousands of other animals have warm blood, too. Some of them are not even in your phylum. Tell what it means to be warm-blooded. Then fill in the missing information about the two warm-blooded classes.

Explain "warm-blooded."

_____

_____

_____

_____

_____

_____

_____ are covered with_____. These are lightweight, flexible, strong coverings which protect the animal from _____ and _____. All of these animals have front limbs called _____. Many, but not all, use these structures to fly. The fertilization of eggs takes place _____ the female's body, but eggs are laid to hatch _____. They breathe with _____ and have a _____–chambered heart. Different birds have different kinds of _____ which are adapted to the kinds of food they eat. Two examples of animals in this class are _____ and _____.

Label each animal shown as
B (bird) or
M (mammal).

_____ have hair to help maintain constant body _____. Females produce _____ to feed to their young. Their hearts have _____ chambers. They also have glands that produce _____ to cool them off when their bodies get too hot. The young of this class develop completely _____ the mother's body before they are born, except in a few cases. Two examples of this class of animals are _____ and _____.

Name _____

CLASS ASSIGNMENTS

You are in the only group of animals that has to go to school. But, like you, all animals have been assigned to classes. Fill in the chart with information to fit each category for each of the 3 fish classes and the other 4 classes of vertebrates.

Class	Kind of Skeleton	# Heart Chambers	Body Covering	Blood Temp.	Where They Live	Where Young Develop	Special Features
JAWLESS FISH							
CARTILAGE FISH							
BONY FISH							
AMPHIBIANS							
REPTILES							
BIRDS							
MAMMALS							

Name

BACKBONE REQUIRED

You have to have a backbone to be able to solve this puzzle. (And, incidentally, all the words in it have something to do with animals that have a backbone of some kind.) Solve the puzzle.

Across

1. bird covering
3. backbone material that is not bone
6. vertebrate class with hair
8. attaches to brain: spinal _____
10. lives partly in water, partly on land
13. system having spinal cord and brain
14. fish egg fertilization is _____
17. class with 3-chambered heart
18. reptile covering

Down

1. chambers in a bird's heart
2. blood of birds and mammals
3. system with heart and vessels
4. breathe with gills
5. bone system in a vertebrate
7. animal group having backbone
9. system which processes food
11. mammal reproduction
    is _____
12. phylum having backbones
15. heart chambers in fish
16. has hollow bones

Name

BEHAVING LIKE ANIMALS

Some beetles stand on their heads. Fiddler crabs change color twice a day. Hognose snakes play dead. Flamingos stand on one leg. African grasshoppers blow bubbles. Some daddy frogs hold tadpoles in their mouths. Spiders spin webs. And Arctic terns fly 11,000 miles for their summer vacation. These are just some of the strange activities that are a part of animal behavior.

Match the behavior-related terms below (A-P) with their descriptions on the right. (If you have some extra time, try to find out why the 8 animals described above do those strange things!)

A. behavior

B. migration

C. territoriality

D. reflex

E. instinct

F. inborn behavior

G. courtship behavior

H. defensive behavior

I. response

J. stimulus

K. trial and error

L. conditioning

M. hibernation

N. camouflage

O. adaptation

P. acquired behavior

_____ 1. an inborn behavior that involves a response to a stimulus

_____ 2. the way an animal acts

_____ 3. behavior learned during life

_____ 4. an action resulting from a stimulus

_____ 5. behavior an animal inherits

_____ 6. quick action not involving the brain

_____ 7. travel to another place to reproduce, avoid cold, find food, or raise young

_____ 8. behavior where animal defends an area

_____ 9. males and females act in certain ways to attract one another for mating

_____ 10. training to cause a certain response to a specific stimulus

_____ 11. an adaptation for winter survival

_____ 12. a change that helps an animal survive in its environment

_____ 13. something that causes a behavior

_____ 14. behavior an animal does to defend itself

_____ 15. changing body coloring that protects an animal

_____ 16. behavior learned based on avoiding mistakes

Name

36

SCALES FOR A CROCODILE?

Why does a crocodile have scales, anyway? Answer these questions to show that you know these animal-related terms.

1. If a crocodile's **scales** are not for weighing, what are they for? _____

   _____

2. An **exoskeleton** is not a group of exercising bones. What is it?_____

   _____

3. Is a **symmetry** a kind of tree? _____What is it?

   _____

4. Is a **spinal cord** anything like a musical chord? _____ Why, or why not?_____

   _____

5. Does a radial tire have **radial symmetry**? _____

   _____

6. Is a jellyfish really a **fish**? _____

   _____

7. If someone has **arachnophobia**, exactly what are they afraid of? _____

8. Is **molt** a kind of **mold**? __ If not, what is it? _____

9. How is a **flagellum** like a flag?_____

   _____

10. **Tentacles** have nothing to do with camping. What are they? _____

    _____

11. What would you find in a cart full of **cartilage**? _____

12. Which is simpler, a **protist** or a **sponge**?_____

13. Is a **cold-blooded** animal more cruel than a **warm-blooded** one? _____

14. Could you fit a **phylum** into a file? _____ Why or why not?_____

15. Does an animal need a generator for **regeneration**?_____

    _____

16. Why might someone scream, "Eeek! An **echinoderm**!" ____

    _____

17. Would you rather hold a handful of **larvae** or **pupae**? Why?

    _____

18. Could you chop wood with a **thorax**? Why or why not? ____

    _____

19. What is "pseudo" (fake) about **pseudopods**? _____

UH-OH, I NEED A NEW SCALE

Name _____

THE HABITAT HABIT

You wouldn't get along too well living in the mud at the bottom of a pond . . . or under the bark of a tree . . . or on the back of a rhinoceros. All living things have this habit of living in a habitat that makes it possible for us to survive. Remember that a habitat is the place in an ecosystem where an organism (and others like it) live and grow.

Describe a habitat which would be suitable for each organism. (Note: Some organisms may be found in more than one habitat. Describe just one.)

1. mosquito _____

2. mushroom _____

3. rattlesnake _____

4. earthworm _____

5. lichen _____

6. ants _____

7. squid _____

8. tree frog _____

9. rhinoceros _____

10. sea cucumber _____

11. roundworm _____

12. mold _____

13. moose _____

14. walrus _____

15. cactus _____

16. trout _____

17. leopard _____

18. antelope _____

19. prairie dog _____

20. alligators _____

21. armadillo _____

22. lizard _____

23. louse _____

24. dog tick _____

25. robin egg _____

26. tapeworm _____

27. mole _____

28. tulip bulb _____

29. fern _____

30. orchid _____

31. hookworm _____

32. brain coral _____

33. fiddler crab _____

Name _____

SOMETHING'S WRONG HERE

The pictures show organisms mixed up about their habitats. Tell what is wrong with each picture, and write a description of what the proper habitat would be for each organism below.

A. _____

C. _____

B. _____

D. _____

F. _____

E. _____

HOME, HOME ON THE BIOME

You probably don't think much about your biome, do you? Maybe if you were a lizard or a coral or a polar bear, you'd be more aware of it. Or, then again, maybe you'd still take your biome for granted.

A **biome** is a region with a distinct climate, a dominant type of plant, and specific organisms which are characteristic to that region. There are 6 major land biomes and 2 major water biomes on the earth.

Use the information in the boxes at the bottom of pages 40 & 41 to do the following tasks. Write your answers in the box for each corresponding biome.

   I. Label the name of each biome.

  II. Write characteristics of each biome.

 III. List some organisms that would be found in that biome.

A.

_____
_____
_____

B.

_____
_____
_____

Biomes	Organisms			
tropical rain forest	leopards	crayfish	lizards	maple trees
temperate deciduous forest	deer	sharks	moose	lions
grassland	parrot	caribou	corals	lichens &
desert	vines	squirrels	cacti	mosses
taiga	sagebrush	prairie dogs	trout	bears
tundra	monkeys	antelope	plankton	sponges
salt water	snakes	polar bears	armadillos	whales
fresh water	ferns	woodpecker	orchids	alligators
	fir trees	palm trees	water lilies	tadpoles
	walrus	grasses	birch trees	cougars
	algae	pondweed	pine trees	penguins
	foxes			

Use with page 41.

Name _____

Use with page 40.

C.

_____
_____
_____

D.

_____
_____
_____

E.

_____
_____
_____

F.

_____
_____
_____

G.

_____
_____
_____

H.

_____
_____
_____

Characteristics of Biomes			
salt water	ponds	permafrost	plentiful rainfall
no trees	fleshy plants	grazing animals	very hot temperatures
little rain	rivers	swamps	large, juicy fruit
streams	sparse plant life	trees lose leaves	irregular precipitation
coniferous forests	marshes	cold desert	plants that store water

Name

EVERYBODY'S IN A CHAIN

Who's eating whom (or what)? That's the big question in a food chain. A **food chain** is a pathway of food and energy through an ecosystem. Each species in the chain depends on the other species in some way. And each species has a role as **producer** (one who makes food) or **consumer** (one who eats food).

    I. Label the role of each organism in these food chains—**producer, primary consumer,** or **secondary consumer.**

A. _____

B. _____

C. _____

D. _____

    II. Label each organism here **producer** (P) or **consumer** (C).

Name _____

WHAT'S WHAT IN THE ECOSYSTEM?

A drop of pond water is one. A whole ocean is one. So is a rotten log in the forest. So is a coral reef and the bark of a tree. **One what?** An **ecosystem!** You might think of an ecosystem as being something huge. But, actually, it can be any size. It is any spot where living organisms are interacting with each other and their nonliving environment. Show how much you know about ecosystems by answering the following questions.

1. What is the difference between a **biosphere** and a **community?** _____

_____

2. Is there only one **population** in a **community?** _____

_____

3. What is a **niche** in a community? _____

_____

4. If you study **ecology**, what are you studying? _____

_____

5. What is the difference between an **environment** and an **ecosystem?** _____

_____

6. When organisms in a community have a **contest** against each other for the life requirements, what are they doing? _____

_____

7. When a raccoon eats a frog, which animal is the **prey?** _____

_____

8. In a relationship of **commensalism**, is either of the two organisms harmed? _____

_____

9. In a **parasitic** relationship, is either of the two organisms harmed? _____

_____

10. What do **decomposers** and **scavengers** have in common? _____

_____

11. What is the first link in every **food chain?** _____

_____

12. What is the difference between a **food web** and a **food chain?** _____

I'M STILL LOOKING FOR MY NICHE

Name _____

RELATIONSHIPS IN THE ECOSYSTEM

It may look as if this bear is simply eating this fish. But it is far from simple. These two animals are in a relationship! Not a very comfortable one for the fish, of course, but an important one in the ecosystem nonetheless!

Use one of the terms at the bottom of the page to label each example described.

1. Vultures gather around a dead deer._____

2. Camels, cacti, sagebrush, lizards, snakes, and insects all live together in a section of desert._____

3. A tick feeds on your dog._____

4. Beetles and termites want to break down the dead material in the same spot on the same dead tree._____

5. Mice feed on acorns; owls feed on mice. _____

6. A pond frog catches a nice fly on his sticky tongue. _____

7. The dandelions seem to be taking over your lawn. _____

8. Mule deer live in the forest behind my house._____

9. A bacteria causes your throat to be sore. _____

10. An orchid attaches itself to a tree branch without doing the tree any harm. _____

11. A poisonous sea anemone gives protection to a fish, but feeds on the predators that come after it. _____

12. A mountain lion stalks a young deer._____

13. A fungus grows on a rotting log. _____

14. Ants crawl all over a dead worm. _____

15. Some bacteria live and get their nourishment inside your intestines, and help to keep them healthy. _____

16. Weeds choke out the young corn plants in your garden. _____

17. A spider traps a fat fly in her web. _____

commensalism
scavengers
community
competition
food chain
mutualism
population
predator-prey
dominant species
decomposer
parasitism
scavenger

Name _____

44

CYCLE CIRCLES

Some major cycles are going on all the time in the ecosystem—affecting the lives of living things. You may not be aware of them, but they just keep going on anyway. The three circles illustrate three major life cycles:

NITROGEN CYCLE   **CARBON DIOXIDE–OXYGEN CYCLE**   **WATER CYCLES**

     I. Label each circle with the name of the cycle.
   II. Label each arrow within each circle.
  III. Beneath each circle, write an explanation of the cycle.

A. _____ CYCLE

B. _____ CYCLE

C. _____ CYCLE

A. _____

_____

_____

_____

B. _____

_____

_____

_____

C. _____

_____

Name

ECO-TALK

This backwards puzzle is loaded with ecology vocabulary. It's "backwards" because the puzzle is already solved. So, instead of solving it, your job is to make up the clues and write them in the appropriate places.

Across

S P E C I E S

²C O N S U M E R

³M U T U A L I S M

⁴C O M P E T I T I O N

⁵N I C H E

⁶S U C C E S S I O N

⁷E C O S Y S T E M

⁸C O M M E N S A L I S M

⁹H A B I T A T

¹⁰B I O S P H E R E

B I O M E

¹¹P R O D U C E R

¹²C H A I N

¹³S C A V E N G E R

¹⁴D O M I N A N T

¹⁵C O M M U N I T Y

¹⁶E C O L O G Y

¹⁷R E S O U R C E

Across

2. _____   15. _____   Down

4. _____   16. _____   1. _____

6. _____   17. _____   3. _____

8. _____   5. _____

10. _____   7. _____

12. _____   9. _____

13. _____   10. _____

14. _____   11. _____

Name

HOW RESOURCEFUL ARE YOU?

This animal is rather resourceful in dealing with a particular **problem** with its air quality. Are you as resourceful in matching the meanings with these terms about **resources**? Tell if each of these words is correctly matched with its meaning by writing **yes** or **no**. If your answer is **no**, give the correct letter for the answer.

yes/no

B _____ 1. acid rain

Q _____ 2. biodegradable

N _____ 3. conservation

P _____ 4. endangered species

D _____ 5. erosion

J _____ 6. extinction

E _____ 7. fossil fuel

L _____ 8. noise pollution

G _____ 9. renewable resources

yes/no

A _____ 10. nonrenewable resources

K _____ 11. pollution

I _____ 12. recycling

M _____ 13. smog

O _____ 14. reforestation

R _____ 15. wildlife preservation

C _____ 16. thermal pollution

F _____ 17. geothermal energy

H _____ 18. sewage

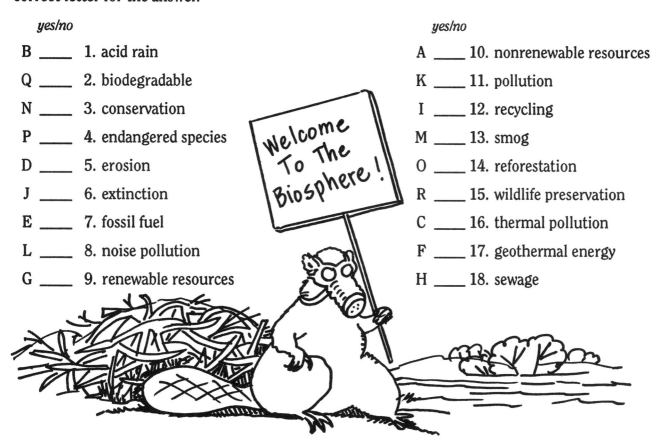

Welcome To The Biosphere!

A. resources that can be replaced by nature

B. nonrenewable fuels formed by millions of years of decay of layers of organisms below the earth's surface

C. pollution where hot water raises the temperature of water in a waterway

D. polluted fog

E. energy obtained from hot spots on or in the earth

F. removal of soil by wind, ice, water, or gravity

G. resources that take hundreds or millions of years to form

H. human waste material

I. renewing a forest by seeding or planting trees

J. adding of impurities to the environment

K. wastes are decomposed by bacteria into materials that do not harm the environment

L. loud or unpleasant sounds

M. water vapor combined with sulfur dioxide in the air

N. wise and careful use of resources

O. no members of a species are left alive

P. only a small number of a species are left

Q. using something over again

R. maintaining living species to protect from extinction

Name _____

UNDER THE MICROSCOPE

You never know what you'll find under the microscope! But to find anything, you need to know how to use one. Label the parts of this light microscope and answer the questions about how it works.

eyepiece

body tube

arm

nosepiece

high power
   objective

low power
   objective

coarse
   adjustment

fine
   adjustment

stage clips

stage

diaphragm

mirror

base

slide

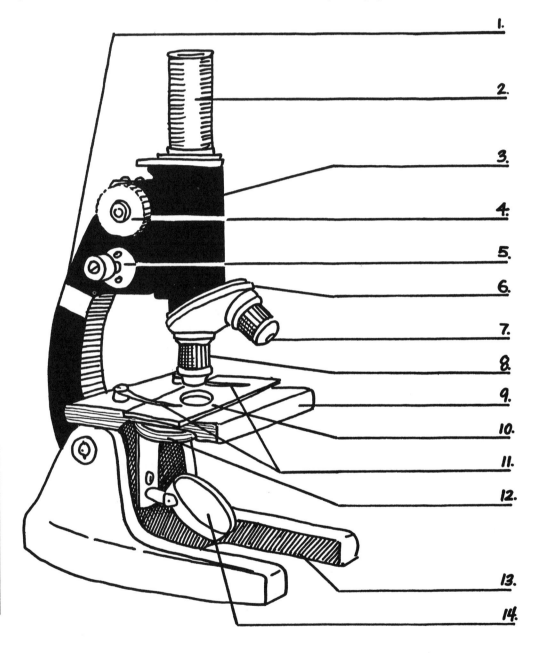

1. _____

2. _____

3. _____

4. _____

5. _____

6. _____

7. _____

8. _____

9. _____

10. _____

11. _____

12. _____

13. _____

14. _____

15. What provides slight focusing to sharpen the image? _____

16. What provides the least magnification? _____

17. What reflects light upwards? _____

18. What regulates the amount of light that enters the body tube? _____

19. What moves the body tube in large movements up and down? _____

20. What holds the microscope slide in place? _____

Name _____

APPENDIX

CONTENTS

Glossary 50

Protist, Moneran, & Fungus Kingdoms 53

Plant Kingdom 54

Animal Kingdom 55

Life Science Skills Test 57

Skills Test Answer Key 61

Answers 62

GLOSSARY

acid rain: type of pollution that forms when sulfur dioxide combines with water vapor in the air

acquired behavior: behavior that is learned

active transport: cell's movement of materials from areas of lower to higher concentration

adaptation: a trait in an organism that increases its ability to survive in its environment

algae: simple plants that have no roots, stems, or leaves and live in or near water

amphibian: cold-blooded animal with moist skin, no scales; lives part of its life in water and part on land

angiosperms: seed plants that produce seeds inside a fruit; flowering plants

annual: a plant that grows, reproduces, and dies in one growing season

anther: part of a plant stamen where pollen forms

arachnid: an arthropod that has two body regions with two pair of jointed structures near the mouth and four pair of legs

bacteria: monerans that cause decomposition

behavior: the reaction of an organism to its environment

biennial: a plant that produces leaves and food in one year; reproduces and dies in the second year

bilateral symmetry: a pattern of symmetry where an object can be divided lengthwise into two like parts

biodegradable: wastes that can be decomposed by bacteria into compounds that do not harm the environment

biome: a region with a distinct climate, dominant plant type, and characteristic organisms

biosphere: a very narrow zone to which life on Earth is limited

bird: warm-blooded vertebrate with feathers

botany: the study of plants

camouflage: body coloring that protects an organism

cartilage: tough, flexible tissue that does not contain all the minerals that make bone stiff; found in joints

cell: basic unit of structure & function in organisms

cell division: the process in which a cell reproduces

cell membrane: the thin layer that surrounds and holds the parts of a cell together

cell wall: rigid layer surrounding outside of plant cell

chlorophyll: the substance that makes a plant green and traps light energy to make food

chloroplasts: cell structures containing chlorophyll

chordate: member of phylum Chordata

circulatory system: a transport system of blood vessels that circulate blood throughout the body

class: a group of organisms smaller than a phylum

classification: way of organizing things into groups

climax community: the last stage in succession

coelenterate: an animal that has a hollow body surrounded by two layers of cells

cold-blooded: having a body temperature that changes with the temperature of the environment

commensalism: a relationship in which one organism lives on another without causing harm

community: all the organisms living together in a certain area

competition: the contest among organisms to obtain all the requirements for life

complete metamorphosis: development in animals with a larva stage that does not resemble the adult

conditioning: training to cause a response to a stimulus that does not normally cause that response

conifers: gymnosperms that form seeds on the upper sides of the woody scales of cones

conservation: wise, careful use of Earth's resources

cotyledons: the seed leaves in the embryo of a seed

crustacean: an animal in phylum Arthropoda that has a segmented body with two main regions

cyanobacteria: monerans that contain the pigment chlorophyll; a main source of food for other organisms

cytoplasm: the jellylike liquid in a cell that contains various cell structures

decomposer: an organism that causes the decay of dead organisms

dicots: flowering plants with flower parts in fours and fives, vascular bundles in a ring inside the stem, and two seed leaves

diffusion: the movement of particles from areas where they are more concentrated to where they are less concentrated

digestion: the process by which food is changed from insoluble to soluble forms

dormancy: a period of time when the plant embryo is in a resting stage

echinoderm: invertebrate that has a mineral skeleton with spines extending out of its body

ecology: the study of the interactions between organisms and their environment

Basic Skills/Life Science 6-8+   Copyright ©1997 by Incentive Publications, Inc., Nashville, TN.

ecosystem: a system in which living organisms interact with each other and their nonliving environment

endangered: only small numbers of a species are living

endoplasmic reticulum: a network of tubelike structures in a cell's cytoplasm

endosperm: food stored in the seeds of monocots

environment: the part of the biosphere that surrounds an organism

epidermis: surface layer of a leaf that protects the inner parts of the leaf

evergreen: trees that keep green leaves all year

exoskeleton: the hard outer covering that protects the internal parts of an arthropod

external fertilization: a process in which sperm fertilizes eggs outside the female animal's body

extinction: the condition occurring when there are no more living members of a species

family: a group of organisms smaller than an order

fish: vertebrate that lives in water and obtains oxygen from the water by using gills

flagellate: whiplike structure some protozoans use for movement

flatworm: a simple animal that has a flat, legless body with identifiable front and rear ends

food chain: the pathway of food and energy through an ecosystem

food web: a complex network of feeding relationships made of many interconnected food chains

fresh water: the biome that includes lakes, swamps, ponds, marshes, and rivers

fungus kingdom: a group of organisms that live in one place and get food from materials they grow on

germination: early growth of a plant from a seed

gills: organs used to obtain oxygen from water

Golgi bodies: structures in a cell's cytoplasm that store and release chemicals in the cell

gymnosperms: seed plants that produce seeds not protected by a fruit

habitat: the place in an ecosystem where populations of organisms live and grow

herbaceous stems: soft, green stems

hibernation: an adaptation for winter survival in which an animals' body functions slow down

homeostasis: the tendency of an organism to adjust itself to maintain a balanced state

inborn behavior: behavior inherited from parents

incomplete metamorphosis: development in animals that involves three stages: egg, nymph, and adult

insect: an arthropod whose body is divided into a head, thorax, and abdomen.

instinct: an inborn behavior that involves complex responses to a stimulus

internal fertilization: a process in which a male deposits sperm inside the female reproductive tract

invertebrate: an animal that has no backbone

leaves: plant organisms that trap light and make food for the plant

mammal: warm-blooded animal that has hair and produces milk to feed its young

metabolism: the sum total of the chemical changes that occur in an organism

metamorphosis: set of stages that occur as certain organisms become adult

mitosis: the process in which a cell's nucleus divides in order to form two new identical cells

mollusks: invertebrate animals that have soft bodies and usually have a shell

moneran: simple 1-celled organism with no nucleus

monocots: flowering plants with flower parts in threes, vascular bundles scattered throughout the stem, and a single seed leaf

mutualism: a relationship in which two organisms live together for mutual benefit

nonrenewable resources: resources that take hundreds or millions of years to form

nonvascular plants: plants without vessels that absorb water through their tissues by osmosis

nucleus: the part of a cell that contains material that controls the activities of the cells

order: a group of organisms smaller than a class

organism: a complete living thing

osmosis: diffusion of water through a membrane

ovary: the lower part of a plant's pistil that produces the ovules containing eggs

ovule: female plant reproductive part; contains egg

parasite: organism that gets food and protection from a host organism, but that also harms the host

perennial: a plant that lives from one growing season to another; includes all woody stem plants

photosynthesis: the process in which plants use light energy to produce food

pistil: female reproductive organ of an angiosperm

plasmolysis: the shrinking of cytoplasm caused by the loss of water

pollen grain: male plant reproductive part that contains sperm

pollination: the transfer of pollen grains to ovules

population: all the organisms of one species in a community

predator: animal that captures another for food

prey: the animals eaten by a predator

producer: organism that contains chlorophyll to make food by photosynthesis

protist: simple, usually 1-celled organism with a nucleus

pseudopods: finger-like projections of cytoplasm used by amoebas to move and obtain food

pupa: the stage of metamorphosis in which the animal forms a covering around itself

radial symmetry: the arrangement of similar parts around a central axis, like the spokes of a wheel

recycling: using over again

regeneration: the regrowth of lost or damaged tissues and organs

renewable resources: resources that can be replaced by nature in a period of time

reproduction: the process in which a living thing produces a new organism like itself

reptile: cold-blooded animal that has scales, breathes air, and lives mainly on land

resource: any source of raw material

respiration: the process by which cells release energy from food molecules for their life activities

response: behavior change caused by a stimulus

rhizoids: hairlike cells that hold liverworts and mosses in the ground and absorb water from soil

roundworm: an invertebrate that has a round, tubelike body that tapers to a point at each end

saprophyte: organism that gets its food from dead organisms or the waste products of living organisms

seed: a fertilized plant ovule

segmented worm: a worm with a tube-shaped body divided into segments that are similar in structure

sepals: leaflike parts of a flowering plant that protect the flower when it is a young bud

skeleton: a frame that shapes, supports, and protects internal organs

species: the smallest category in a kingdom in which only one kind of an organism is classified

spore: reproductive cell; grows into an organism

sporophyte: plant life cycle stage that forms spores

stamens: the male reproductive organs of angiosperms

stigma: the part of the pistil with a sticky tip upon which pollen grains land

stimulus: something in the environment that causes a behavior

stomata: the slitlike openings or pores in a leaf

style: the stalk of a pistil

succession: the gradual change in a community over time

symmetry: a similarity or likeness of parts

system: a group of organs that work together to carry on life activities

taiga: a biome that lies north of the temperate region and is covered mostly by great coniferous forests

taxonomy: the science of classifying living things

tentacle: a ropelike piece of tissue used by some animals to obtain food

territoriality: a behavior in which an animal defends a particular area or territory

tissue: a group of cells with a similar shape and function that together perform a specific job

transpiration: loss of water vapor through stomata of a leaf

trial and error: a type of conditioned learning in which an animal develops a behavior based on avoiding mistakes

tube feet: structures in rows on the underside of an echinoderm that work like suction cups

tundra: a biome that lies south of the Arctic Ocean and within the polar regions where the ground remains frozen most of the year

vacuole: a liquid-filled sac in a cell that stores water and dissolved materials

vertebrate: an animal with a backbone

virus: a complex organic compound that has properties of both living and nonliving things

warm-blooded: maintaining a nearly constant body temperature despite the surroundings

water vascular system: a system that echinoderms use to move and obtain food

wildlife preservation: the maintaining of living species to protect them from extinction

wildlife refuge: area in which wildlife and their habitats are protected

woody stems: hard, rigid stems

zoology: the study of animals

PROTIST KINGDOM

The Protist kingdom is made up of several phyla, including euglenoids, golden algae, slime molds, sporozoans, ciliates, flagellates, dinoflagellates, and sarcodines. Protists are mostly one-celled organisms, although slime molds can have many cells. Some make their own food, but most take in or absorb food. Many have one or two flagella, cilia, or pseudopods that enable them to move. Sporozoans have no means of movement.

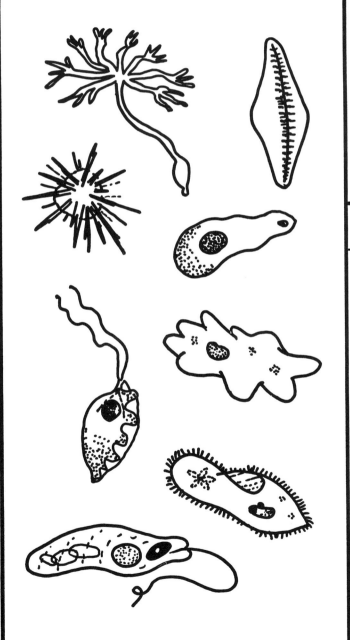

MONERAN KINGDOM

The Moneran kingdom is made up of two phyla: cyanobacteria and bacteria. Both are one-celled organisms, though some cyanobacteria hang together in colonies. Cyanobacteria make their own food, contain chlorophyll, and are mostly blue-green in color. Bacteria mostly absorb food and some contain chlorophyll. Bacteria can be round, rod-shaped, or spiral in shape.

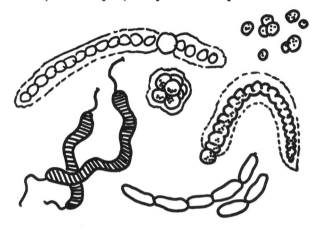

FUNGUS KINGDOM

The Fungus kingdom has three phyla. Sac fungi can be one or many cells. The spores are produced in a small sac called an ascus. Club fungi have many cells and produce spores in club-shaped sacs called basidia. Sporangium fungi have many cells and produce spores in sporangia. All fungi absorb food.

PLANT KINGDOM

GREEN ALGAE

These are one-celled plants living in colonies, or many-celled, green, nonvascular plants living in water or on land. They make their own food and form zygospores for reproduction.

BROWN ALGAE

These are many-celled, brown, nonvascular plants. They make their own food and live mostly in salt water.

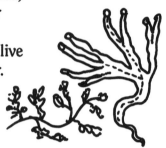

RED ALGAE

These are many-celled, red, nonvascular plants. They make their own food and live mostly in deep salt water.

LIVERWORTS & MOSSES

These are many-celled, green, nonvascular plants. They make their own food and have a root system of rhizoids. They grow in moist areas on land and reproduce from spores in capsules.

CLUB MOSSES & HORSETAILS

These plants are vascular and have many cells. They live on land. They are green and make their own food. They form spores in cones.

FERNS

Ferns are many-celled, vascular plants. They are green and make their own food. They have feathery leaves called fronds. They live on land or in water and produce spores in sporangia.

GYMNOSPERMS

These are seed plants which produce seeds in cones. They are many-celled, vascular, and make their own food. They live on land.

ANGIOSPERMS

These are seed plants that produce flowers and seeds in fruits. They are many-celled, vascular, and make their own food. They live on land.

ANIMAL KINGDOM

PHYLUM PORIFERA
(sponges)

These are a thick sack of cells that form pores, chambers, or canals. They live in water and attach themselves to one place where they stay.

PHYLUM COELENTERATA
(coelenterates)

These have a central cavity with a mouth. Most have tentacles. They live in water. Some are attached to one spot.

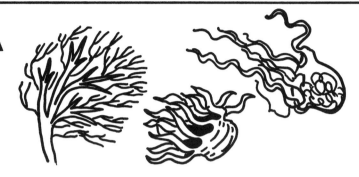

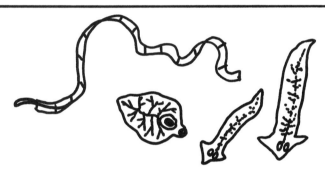

PHYLUM PLATYHELMINTHES
(flatworms)

These are flat-bodied worms that live as parasites or move freely in water.

PHYLUM NEMATODA
(roundworms)

These are round-bodied worms that live as parasites or move freely in water or on land.

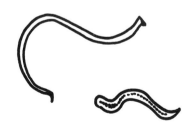

PHYLUM ANNELIDA
(segmented worms)

These worms have bodies that are divided into segments. All the segments have bristles. They live on land or in water. They are not parasitic.

Basic Skills/Life Science 6-8+

PHYLUM MOLLUSCA (mollusks)

Mollusks have soft bodies with hard or shell coverings. They live on land or in water. Many of them have a thick, muscular foot for movement. Some live attached to surfaces such as rocks.

PHYLUM ARTHROPODA (arthropods)

Arthropods have bodies divided into segments. Their legs are jointed, and they have hard exoskeletons made of chitin. The exoskeletons are hinged to allow movement. Arthropods shed their exoskeletons from time to time in order to grow. They live on land or in water.

PHYLUM ECHINODERMATA (echinoderms)

Echinoderms are animals with radial symmetry. They have a tough, outer covering that is covered with spines. All echinoderms live in salt water and have a water vascular system for movement. They also have structures called tube feet which attach to objects for movement.

PHYLUM CHORDATA (chordates)

Chordates are distinguished by their internal skeletons made of bones or cartilage. They also have specialized body systems for digestion, circulation, and a central nervous system. Vertebrates may live on land or in water.

56

LIFE SCIENCE
SKILLS TEST

Write the correct answer to each question in its corresponding blank.

_____ 1. Which is **not** a characteristic of all living organisms?
a. ability to move   b. needs water   c. gives off waste   d. is made of cells

_____ 2. What part of the cell controls movement of materials in and out of the cell?

_____ 3. In what cell structure are proteins made?
a. mitochondria   b. Golgi bodies   c. ribosomes   d. nucleus

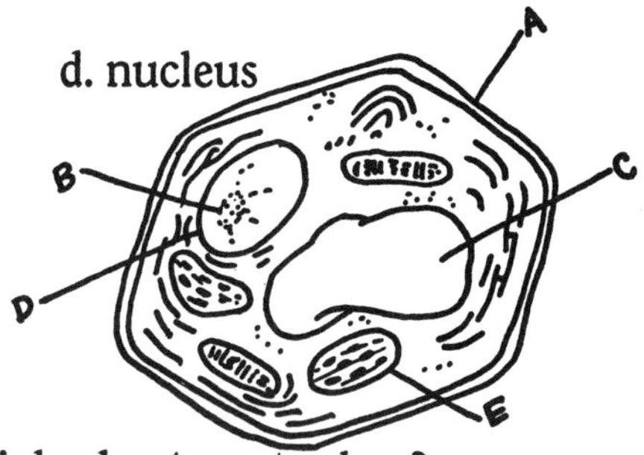

_____ 4. What structure in a plant cell contains chlorophyll?

_____ 5. What kind of a cell is pictured here: plant or animal?

_____ 6. Which part of the pictured cell regulates the movement of materials in and out of the nucleus?

_____ 7. Which part of the pictured cell stores water and dissolved materials?

_____ 8. What process is happening when a cell's cytoplasm shrinks due to water loss?
a. metabolism   b. active transport   c. mitosis   d. plasmolysis

_____ 9. During what process do plants release energy from stored food?
a. feedback   b. photosynthesis   c. respiration   d. diffusion

_____ 10. What process is the tendency of an organism to adjust itself to maintain a balanced state?

_____ 11. What is the basic unit of structure and function in all organisms?

_____ 12. A(n) _____ is a trait whereby an organism changes to survive changes in its environment.

_____ 13. What is the smallest division of a kingdom for classification of living things?

_____ 14. Water passes through a cell membrane by
a. photosynthesis   b. respiration   c. adaptation   d. osmosis

_____ 15. The part of a compound microscope that moves the body tube up and down for focusing is the _____ .

_____ 16. The part of a compound microscope that holds a slide in place is the _____ .

_____ 17. What kingdom is represented by E (pictured at the right)?

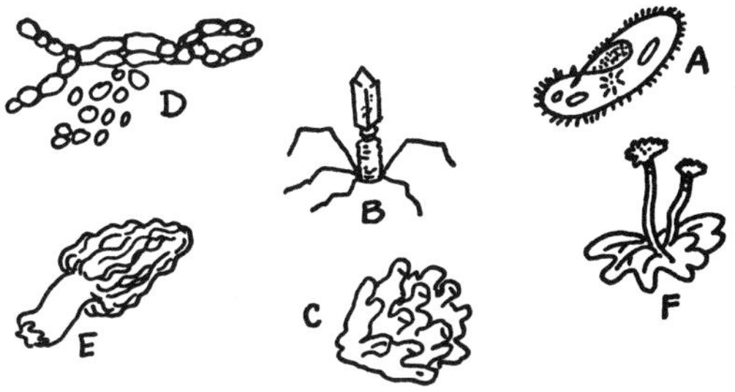

_____ 18. Which organism pictured belongs to the protist kingdom?

_____ 19. Which organism pictured belongs to the animal kingdom?

_____ 20. What short, hairlike structures help some protists move?

_____ 21. Which of these have properties of both living and nonliving things?
a. bacteria   b. viruses   c. fungi   d. protists

_____ 22. Which of the simple organisms pictured below are **neither** fungi **nor** protists?

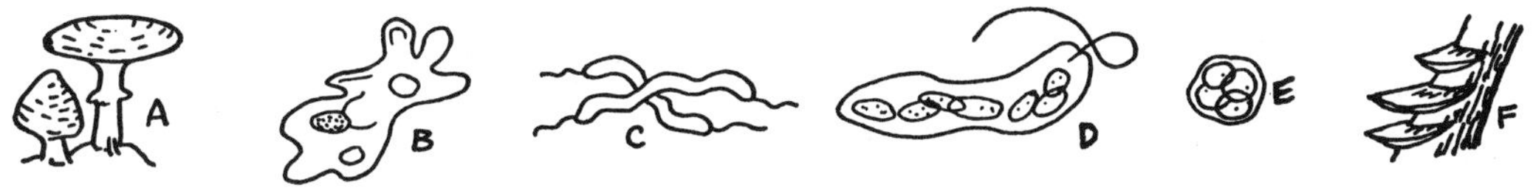

Name

Basic Skills/Life Science 6-8+

_____ 23. What is added to the atmosphere during respiration?

_____ 24. A plant that has tubelike structures to carry water and nutrients is a(n) ___ plant.

_____ 25. A plant that grows, reproduces, and dies within one season is a(n) _____ plant.

_____ 26. During the process of _____ , water is lost through the stomata in plant leaves.

_____ 27. A(n) _____ is a young plant growing within a seed.

_____ 28. Fir, pine, spruce, and redwood trees are
a. angiosperms   b. gymnosperms   c. nonvascular plants   d. deciduous

_____ 29. Plants get the nitrogen they need from _____ .

_____ 30. The part of the flower that produces pollen is the _____ .

_____ 31. The _____ is the female reproductive organ of a flowering plant.

_____ 32. Most of the oxygen in the atmosphere comes from
a. evaporation   b. diffusion   c. transpiration   d. photosynthesis

_____ 33. The ____ is the part of the plant that traps light energy for use in photosynthesis.

_____ 34. In the flower pictured at right, A is the _____ .

_____ 35. Which letter labels the flower part that will develop into a fruit?

_____ 36. Which letter labels the male reproductive organ?

_____ 37. Animals with backbones belong to what phylum?

_____ 38. Which animals pictured below are invertebrates?

_____ 39. Starfish and sand dollars belong to the _____ phylum.

_____ 40. Jellyfish and coral belong to the same phylum as
a. snails   b. sponges   c. sea anemones   d. fish

_____ 41. An animal belonging to the phylum arthropoda is a
a. tapeworm   b. lobster   c. squid   d. slug

_____ 42. An animal that is **not** a mollusk is a
a. clam   c. slug
b. octopus   d. sea cucumber

_____ 43. Which organism(s) pictured at right has(ve) **no** symmetry?

_____ 44. Which organism(s) pictured at right has(ve) **radial** symmetry?

_____ 45. Which organism(s) pictured above has(ve) **bilateral** symmetry?

_____ 46. _____ animals keep a constant body temperature.

_____ 47. _____ are structures that help fish get oxygen from water.

_____ 48. The number of body segments that insects have is _____ .

_____ 49. _____ is the process where insects shed their exoskeletons as they grow.

_____ 50. The bodies of mammals are covered with _____ .

_____ 51. Animals in the _____ phylum have jointed legs.

_____ 52. _____ is the class of arthropods which have 8 legs.

_____ 53. Which animal (at right) is a coelenterate?

_____ 54. Which animal (at right) is a sponge?

Name

_____ 55. In the examples shown below, to what phylum does B belong?
a. segmented worm   b. roundworm   c. flatworm   d. echinoderm

_____ 56. In the examples below, which animal has bilateral symmetry?

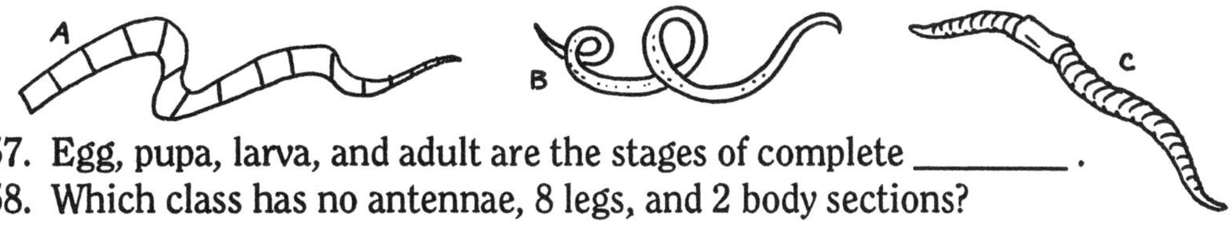

_____ 57. Egg, pupa, larva, and adult are the stages of complete _____ .

_____ 58. Which class has no antennae, 8 legs, and 2 body sections?
a. fish   c. arachnids
b. crustaceans   d. insects

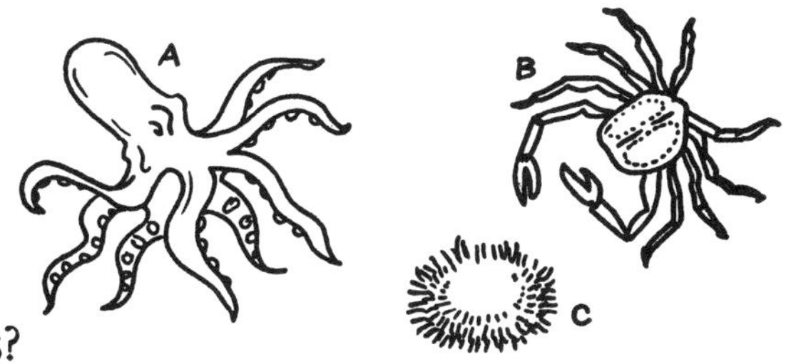

_____ 59. Which animal (at right) is an arthropod?

_____ 60. Which animal (at right) is a mollusk?

_____ 61. Which animal (at right) has radial symmetry?

_____ 62. Which is **not** a characteristic of mammals?
a. hair covering   b. 3-chambered heart   c. produce milk   d. produce sweat

_____ 63. Which is **not** a characteristic of birds?
a. 4-chambered heart   b. hollow bones   c. cold-blooded   d. lungs

_____ 64. Which is **not** a characteristic of reptiles?
a. exoskeleton   b. backbone   c. scale covering   d. cold-blooded

_____ 65. Which organism undergoes complete metamorphosis?
a. fish   b. frog   c. grasshopper   d. moth

_____ 66. What class of arthropods has 2 pair of antennae, gills, and a flexible exoskeleton?

_____ 67. Which animal pictured below is a millipede?

_____ 68. Which animal pictured below is a crustacean?

_____ 69. E (pictured below) belongs to what class of arthropod?

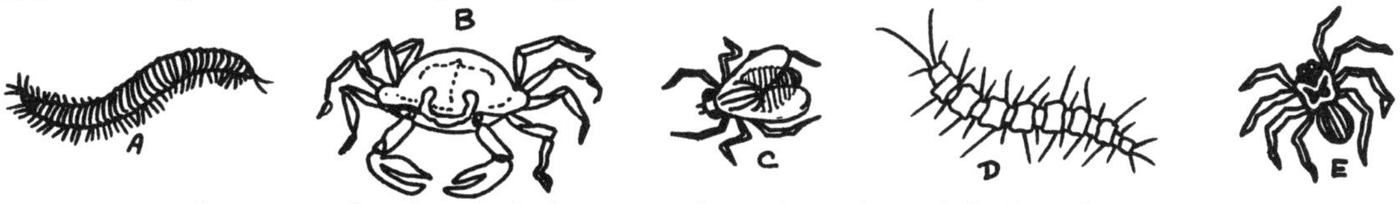

_____ 70. In the row of animals below, to what class does A belong?

_____ 71. Which animals below are **not** warm-blooded?

_____ 72. Which animal pictured below has gills and lungs?

_____ 73. A _____ is a place in the ecosystem where populations of organisms live and grow.

_____ 74. Organisms that remove and eat dead organisms are called _____ .

_____ 75. A _____ is all the organisms of one species in a community.

_____ 76. Which of these represents an ecosystem?
a. a dead tree   c. a coral reef
b. a drop of pond water   d. all of these

_____ 77. The picture on the right represents which biome?
a. taiga   c. desert
b. tundra   d. temperate forest

Name _____

Basic Skills/Life Science 6-8+   Copyright ©1997 by Incentive Publications, Inc., Nashville, TN.

_____ 78. A _____ is the role an organism plays in a community.

_____ 79. The first link in a food chain is always

       a. grass   b. a producer   c. a primary consumer   d. a secondary consumer

_____ 80. The part of the biosphere that surrounds an organism is its _____ .

_____ 81. What kind of resources are coal, petroleum, and natural gas?

_____ 82. If a species is _____ , its organisms are found in very small numbers.

_____ 83. A complex network of food relationships is called a _____ .

_____ 84. A biome that supports large herds of animals is _____ .

_____ 85. Which would **not** be found in a temperate deciduous forest?

       a. coral   b. maple trees   c. deer   d. insects

_____ 86. Which would **not** be found in a taiga biome?

       a. pine trees   c. fir trees

       b. permafrost   d. moose and bears

_____ 87. Which organisms in these food chains (at right) are primary consumers?

_____ 88. Which organisms in these food chains are producers?

_____ 89. Which organisms in these food chains are secondary consumers?

_____ 90. An orchid lives on a tree without causing the tree harm. This is _____ .

       a. predatorism   b. parasitism   c. commensalism   d. pollination

_____ 91. A fungus causes the decay of a dead log. The fungus is a _____ .

       a. decomposer   b. scavenger   c. competitor   d. predator

_____ 92. Some fish and sea anemone live together in a relationship that benefits both. This is called _____ .

       a. parasitism   b. mutualism   c. commensalism   d. competition

_____ 93. Sulfur dioxide combines with water vapor in the air to produce a pollutant called _____ .

_____ 94. Animals and crops raised for food and trees are examples of _____ resources.

_____ 95. Which organisms pictured above are consumers?

_____ 96. Ash, dust, smog, acid rain, noise, and auto exhaust are all examples of _____ .

_____ 97. _____ is the renewing of a forest by planting new trees or seeds.

_____ 98. _____ substances are organic wastes that are **not** harmful to the environment when decomposed.

_____ 99. Are wood and coal both fossil fuels?

_____100. _____ pollution raises the temperature of water in waterways.

SCORE: Total Points _____ out of a possible 100 points

Name _____

LIFE SCIENCE
SKILLS TEST ANSWER KEY

1. a
2. cell membrane
3. c
4. chloroplast
5. plant
6. D
7. C
8. d
9. c
10. homeostasis
11. cell
12. adaptation
13. species
14. d
15. coarse adjustment
16. stage clips
17. fungus
18. A
19. C
20. cilia
21. b
22. C and D
23. carbon dioxide
24. vascular
25. annual
26. transpiration
27. embryo
28. b
29. soil
30. anther
31. pistil
32. d
33. leaf (or chlorophyll)
34. stigma

35. C
36. B
37. chordata
38. C, D, E, H
39. echinodermata
40. c
41. b
42. d
43. C
44. A
45. B and D
46. warm-blooded
47. gills
48. three
49. molting
50. hair
51. arthropod
52. arachnid
53. A
54. C
55. b
56. A
57. metamorphosis
58. c
59. B
60. A
61. A
62. b
63. c
64. a
65. d
66. crustaceans
67. A
68. B

69. arachnid
70. fish
71. A, C, D, F
72. C
73. community
74. scavengers
75. population
76. d
77. b
78. niche
79. b
80. environment
81. nonrenewable
82. endangered
83. food web
84. grassland
85. a
86. b
87. mouse and small fish
88. acorn and sea plants
89. owl, big fish, person
90. c
91. a
92. b
93. acid rain (or snow)
94. renewable
95. B and D
96. pollution
97. reforestation
98. biodegradable
99. no
100. thermal

ANSWERS

Page 10

(Answers 1-7 may vary slightly in explanation.)
1. has a life span during which it grows, develops, and dies
2. is made up of cells
3. uses energy
4. needs water
5. responds to changes in its environment
6. gives off waste products
7. reproduces new organisms like itself
8. organism
9. cell
10-12. carbon, hydrogen, oxygen
13. 70%
14. circulate
15. wastes
16. energy
17. adaptation
18. tissue
19. organ
20. system

Page 11

1. diffusion
2. plasmolysis
3. mitosis
4. osmosis
5. metabolism
6. cell division
7. respiration
8. homeostasis
9. active transport
10. homeostasis
11. diffusion
12. mitosis
13. metabolism

Pages 12-13

I. 1. cell membrane
    2. nuclear membrane
    3. nucleus
    4. chromosomes
    5. cytoplasm
    6. mitochondria
    7. Golgi bodies
    8. nuclear membrane
    9. chromosomes
    10. nucleus
    11. cell membrane
    12. mitochondria
    13. chloroplast
    14. vacuole
    15. Golgi bodies
    16. cell wall

II. A. animal cell
     B. plant cell

III.
1. K	4. B	7. D	10. G
2. A	5. E	8. H	11. F
3. C	6. L	9. I	12. J

Page 14

1. animal kingdom
2. plant kingdom
3. fungus kingdom
4. protist kingdom
5. moneran kingdom
6. protist
7. plant, fungus, moneran
8. animal
9. protist, animal
10. moneran
11. plant, fungus
12. moneran
13. plant
14. animal, fungus
15. protist, moneran
16. phylum, class, order, family, genus, species

Page 15

1. no	11. no
2. no	12. yes
3. an organism	13. moneran
4. microscope	14. saprophyte
5. yes	15. yes
6. (vary) insects, air, water, food	16. no
	17. yes
7. no	18. no
8. both	19. pasteuriza-
9. interferon	tion
10. (vary) some are polio, rubella, yellow fever, smallpox, influenza	20. spirilla
	21. bocci
	22. bacilli
	23. mutualism
	24. parasitism

Page 16

1. T	5. F	9. F	13. F
2. T	6. F	10. T	14. F
3. F	7. F	11. T	15. T
4. T	8. F	12. T	16. F

Page 17

1. plant organ that traps light and makes food for the plant
2. plant tissue that transports water around the plant
3. system where food is stored in a thick, long, main root
4. thin layer of brick-shaped cells that cover and protect the surface of the leaf
5. waxy covering of the leaf epidermis
6. plant tissue that transports food from leaves to other plant parts
7. tubelike structures that transport water and nutrients around the plant
8. plant growth tissue that makes new xylem and phloem cells
9. part of the leaf that traps sunlight
10. tiny openings in epidermis of leaf that let things pass in & out
11. leaf stalk that attaches leaf to stem in many plants
12. root system with many branches
13. threadlike cells that bring water and nutrients into root
14. structures that anchor plants into the ground and take in water and nutrients
15. B
16. A

Page 18

(Answers will vary somewhat.)

PHOTOSYNTHESIS

Green plants trap and use energy from light to make food. The chlorophyll in the green plant cells are what traps the light. The plant combines carbon dioxide and water to produce sugar and oxygen. Energy is stored in the food (sugar); some oxygen is released into the air. This is the opposite of respiration.

RESPIRATION

Respiration is opposite from photosynthesis. In respiration, energy is released from food. The plant uses oxygen to breakdown sugar so the plant can use the energy for its life processes. Water and carbon dioxide are released as this process takes place.

GAS EXCHANGE

Tiny openings in the leaf epidermis, called stomata, allow gases to pass in and out of the leaf by diffusion. The gases that move in and out are oxygen, carbon dioxide, and water vapor. The stomata are usually open during the day and closed at night.

TRANSPIRATION

Plants lose water vapor through the stomata in the leaves. A plant takes in water through its roots and loses a substantial amount of water through transpiration each day.

Page 19

Corrected version of story:

I'm the really important part of the whole plan! I carry pollen grains from the anthers on top of the filaments of the stamen on one flower and leave them on the sticky stigma (which is part of the pistil) of another.

After I leave this stuff on the sticky stigma, a sepal grows down through the petal toward the ovule. The sperm passes out of the pollen tube into the egg and fertilizes it.

The fertilized seed develops into an embryo, and the wall of the surrounding ovary develops into a fruit. When the fruit bursts open or is thrown on the ground, the seeds fall into the ground and start new plants.

1. stigma	7. ovule
2. style	8. ovary
3. pistil	9. filament
4. petal	10. anther
5. embryo	11. stamen
6. sepal	12. pollen

Pages 20-21

A. 9	K. 11	U. 27
B. 1	L. 24	V. 29
C. 12	M. 23	W. 22
D. 16	N. 28	X. 25
E. 20	O. 19	Y. 17
F. 30	P. 8	Z. 14
G. 26	Q. 5	AA. 6
H. 13	R. 2	BB. 10
I. 3	S. 15	XX. 4
J. 18	T. 21	ZZ. 7

Page 22

BONES:
1, 3, 4, 7, 8, 10, 11, 14, 19, 20, 21, 22, 23, 26, 27, 28, 29, 31, 32
NO BONES:
2, 5, 6, 9, 12, 13, 15, 16, 17, 18, 24, 25, 30

Page 23

1. B	8. N	15. R
2. B	9. R	16. R
3. B	10. B	17. B
4. B	11. B	18. B
5. R	12. R	19. B
6. R	13. R	20. N
7. B	14. R	

His body has bilateral symmetry.

Page 24

PORIFERA: elephant ear sponge ..(A)
PLATYHELMINTHES: tapeworm ..(H)
COELENTERATA: jellyfish ....(D)
NEMOTODA: hookworm................(I)
MOLLUSCA: octopus, clam ....(B)
ANNELIDA: bristleworm,
     earthworm ....(G)
ECHINODERMATA: sea urchin .....(C)
ARTHROPODA: ant, bee, shrimp ..(E)
CHORDATA: hawk, gull, frog, ray .(F)

Page 26

Descriptions will vary.

1. coelenterates—live in water, some float, some are attached; have a central cavity and a mouth; most have tentacles
2. flatworms—live in water or attached to other organism as a parasite; have flattened body
3. roundworms—live in water or on land or attached to other organism as a parasite; have round body
4. segmented worms—live in water or on land; body is divided into segments; body segments have bristles
5. sponges—live in water, stay attached to one place; are made of a thick sack of cells with canals, chambers, or pores

Page 27

I.
1. E	5. M	9. M	13. M
2. M	6. E	10. E	14. E
3. M	7. B	11. M	15. M
4. M	8. E	12. M	16. B

II.
A. M	D. M	G. M
B. M	E. M	H. E
C. E	F. M	I. E

Page 28

ALL ARTHROPODS: .... f, h, s
MILLIPEDES: .... k, o, u
CENTIPEDES: .... c, j, k, v
CRUSTACEANS: ... a, i, l, p, r, t, x
ARACHNIDS: .... g, p, q, n
INSECTS: .... b, d, e, k, m, w

Page 29

1. 2
2. 2
3. 0
4. 4
5. biting and chewing
6. land
7. a, b, e, f, h, i, j
8. c, d, g, k

Page 30

I.
1. F	5. T	9. T	13. T
2. T	6. F	10. T	
3. T	7. F	11. T	
4. F	8. F	12. T	

II. hermit crab   millipede
    centipede   shrimp
    spider   crayfish
    spider   spider

Page 31

1. set of stages that occur as some organisms grow into adults
2. 1) egg 2) larva 3) pupa 4) adult
3. the egg grows into a nymph that looks like a miniature adult; as the nymph grows, it molts several times and grows larger, and sometimes adds wings. At the end of all the molting stages, it becomes an adult.
4. (vary) bees, ants, flies, fleas, moths, etc.
5. (vary) grasshopper, termite, cockroach, dragonfly, etc.
6. the animal sheds its exoskeleton
7. A. the monarch
8. B. the grasshopper

butterfly:...........A. eggs   B. larva
                C. pupa   D. adult
grasshopper: .....E. eggs   F. nymph
                G. adult

Page 32

A cold-blooded animal has a body temperature that changes with the temperature of the environment.

1. fish
2. water
3. gills
4. three
5. jawless
6. cartilage
7. bony
8. eggs
9-10. Answers will vary.
11. amphibians
12-13. land, water
14. water
15. land
16. moist
17. air
18. gills
19. develop or grow
20. hatch
21. three
22-23. Answers will vary.
24. reptiles
25. air
26. land
27. scales
28. three
29. eggs
30-31. Answers will vary.
F—fish;
A—frog;
R—turtle, snake

Page 33

A warm-blooded animal maintains a nearly constant body temperature despite its surroundings.

1. birds
2. feathers
3-4. hot, cold
5. wings
6. inside
7. outside
8. lungs
9. four
10. beaks
11-12. Answers will vary.
13. mammals
14. temperature
15. milk
16. four
17. sweat
18. inside
19-20. Answers will vary.
B—all birds shown;
M—monkey, bat

Page 34

CLASS	Kind of Skeleton	# Heart Chmbrs.	Body Covering	Blood Temp.	Where They Live	Where Young Develop	Special Features
JAWLESS FISH	cartilage	2	scales	cold	fresh or salt water	external in eggs	gills, sucker-mouths
CARTILAGE FISH	cartilage	2	scales	cold	mostly salt water	external in eggs	gills, hinged jaws
BONY FISH	bones	2	scales	cold	fresh or salt water	external in eggs	gills, fins, hinged jaws
AMPHIBIANS	bones	3	moist skin	cold	land or water	external in eggs	can breathe in water or on land
REPTILES	bones	3	scales	cold	mainly on land	external in eggs	never has feathers
BIRDS	bones	4	feathers	warm	land, water, air	external in eggs	hollow bones, wings
MAMMALS	bones	4	hair	warm	mostly land	mostly internal	produce milk, sweat

Page 35

Page 36

1. E	5. F	9. G	13. J
2. A	6. D	10. L	14. H
3. P	7. B	11. M	15. N
4. I	8. C	12. O	16. K

Page 37

1. prevent loss of water from body
2. a hard outer covering that protects the inside parts of an arthropod
3. no; similarity or likeness of parts

4. Answers will vary.
5. yes
6. no; it is in a different phylum—coelenterate
7. creatures with 2 body parts, 8 legs, no antennae—a kind of arthropod
8. no; the process of shedding the exoskeleton
9. it is long and skinny and waves around
10. ropelike tissue on some animals; used to obtain food
11. tough, flexible tissue found in joints; not as stiff as bone
12. protist
13. not necessarily
14. no; a phylum is a large group of animals
15. no; they just do it on their own
16. maybe because of the spines sticking out, or the weird looks
17. pupae; larvae are too squirmy (answers may vary)
18. no; it is not an axe, it is the middle section of a body
19. they are not real feet, they just work like feet

Page 38

Answers will vary. Accept any reasonable answer.

Page 39

Accept reasonable answers and explanations about what is wrong with each example.

Pages 40-41

A. fresh water biome: algae, trout, tadpoles, streams, ponds, rivers, water lilies, marsh, swamp, crayfish, alligators, snakes, pondweeds

B. salt water biome: corals, whales, sponges, sharks, plankton

C. tropical rainforest biome: vines, palm trees, ferns, parrots, monkeys, orchids, plentiful rainfall, large juicy fruit, very hot temperatures, snakes, leopards

D. taiga biome: deer, fir trees, foxes, squirrels, woodpecker, moose, pine trees, bears, coniferous forests

E. temperate deciduous forest biome: deer, bears, foxes, squirrels, woodpeckers, birch trees, maple trees, trees that lose leaves

F. tundra biome: grasses, lichens and mosses, polar bears, permafrost, caribou, walrus, no trees, cold desert, penguins, sparse plant life, swamps

G. grassland biome: antelope, prairie dogs, grasses, grazing animals, cougars, lions, irregular precipitation

H. desert biome: lizards, snakes, cacti, sagebrush, armadillos, little rain, fleshy plants, plants that store water

Page 42

I. A. owl—secondary consumer; mouse—primary consumer; acorns—producer
B. pelican—secondary consumer; fish—primary consumer; plants—producer
C. fox—secondary consumer; rabbit—primary consumer; plants—producer
D. people—secondary consumer; sheep—primary consumer; grass—producer

II.
1. C   5. C   9. P
2. C   6. P   10. C
3. C   7. P
4. P   8. C

Page 43

1. biosphere is the space around the earth where organisms can live; a community is all the organisms that live in a certain area
2. usually there are many populations
3. the role of an organism in a community
4. interactions between organisms and their environment
5. ecosystem has to do with the interactions between organisms; environment is the surroundings of an organism
6. competing
7. frog
8. no
9. yes
10. they both hang around dead organisms
11. a producer
12. a food chain is a pathway of food and energy; a food web is a complex network of food relationships which includes many food chains

Page 44

1. scavengers
2. community
3. parasitism
4. competition
5. food chain; predator-prey
6. predator-prey
7. dominant species
8. population
9. parasitism
10. commensalism
11. mutualism
12. predator-prey
13. decomposer
14. scavengers
15. mutualism
16. competition
17. predator-prey

Page 45

(Explanations and labels may vary slightly.)

A. WATER CYCLE
Labels:
up arrow—evaporation;
down arrow: precipitation.

All organisms need water. There is a constant cycle of water in the environment. Water evaporates from the surfaces of rivers, lakes, oceans, and soil. Plants give off water during transpiration. Water vapor in the air forms clouds and returns to the earth as rain, snow, or other precipitation.

B. NITROGEN CYCLE
Labels: down arrow: soil bacteria remove nitrogen from air; up arrow: nitrogen returned to air by dying organisms.

Bacteria in the soil remove nitrogen from the air and combine it with oxygen to make nitrates. Plants can absorb these nitrates and use them to make compounds that animals need. Animals take in the nitrates through these compounds (such as proteins). When plants and animals die, they decompose and return these nitrates to the soil. Bacteria in the soil break them down and return nitrogen to the air.

C. CARBON DIOXIDE-OXYGEN CYCLE
top arrow: oxygen from plants;
bottom arrow: carbon dioxide from animals.

Plants and animals need carbon dioxide and oxygen. Plants and animals take in oxygen and give off carbon dioxide as they breathe. Plants remove carbon dioxide during photosynthesis and return oxygen to the air. Plants and animals are continuously exchanging the oxygen and carbon dioxide that they need.

Page 46

Across
2. eats other organisms
4. contest among organisms
6. gradual change in a community over time
8. one organism lives off another without harm
10. narrow zone on Earth that supports life
12. pathway of food through ecosystem: food ____
13. removes and eats dead animals
14. most prevalent species in an area
15. all organisms living together in an area
16. study of interactions between organisms and environment
17. any source of raw material

Down
1. smallest category of classification of living things
3. two organisms live together for mutual benefit
5. role of an organism in the community
7. system where living and nonliving things interact
9. place in ecosystem where population lives
10. region with a distinct climate, dominant plant type, and distinctive organisms
11. contains chlorophyll to make food for itself and other organisms

Page 47

1. no—M
2. no—K
3. yes—N
4. yes—P
5. no—F
6. no—O
7. no—B
8. yes—L
9. no—A
10. no—G
11. no—J
12. no—Q
13. no—D
14. no—I
15. yes—R
16. yes—C
17. no—E
18. yes—H

Page 48

1. arm
2. eyepiece
3. body tube
4. coarse adjustment
5. fine adjustment
6. nosepiece
7. low power objective
8. high power objective
9. stage
10. slide
11. stage clips
12. diaphragm
13. base
14. mirror
15. fine adjustment
16. low power objective
17. mirror
18. diaphragm
19. coarse adjustment
20. stage clips